The Little Book *of* Prayers

EDITED BY DAVID SCHILLER

WORKMAN PUBLISHING · NEW YORK

For Ruth

Copyright © 1996 by David Schiller

All rights reserved. No portion of this book may be reproduced—
mechanically, electronically, or by any other means, including photocopying—
without written permission of the publisher. Published simultaneously in
Canada by Thomas Allen & Son Limited.

The scripture excerpt on pages 32–33 is from the Revised Standard Version
of the Bible; all other excerpts are from the King James Version.

Additional credits and acknowledgments start on page 384,
and constitute an extension of this copyright notice.

The Library of Congress has catalogued the previous format of
this book as follows:

The little book of prayers/[edited] by David Schiller.
p. cm
ISBN 0-7611-0453-4
1. Prayers I. Schiller, David.
BL560.L584   1996
291.4'3—dc20   96-10866
                                     CIP
ISBN 978-0-7611-7758-6 (new format)

Revised design by Janet Vicario

Workman books are available at special discounts when purchased in bulk
for premiums and sales promotions as well as for fund-raising or educational
use. Special editions or book excerpts also can be created to specification.
For details, contact the Special Sales Director at the address below,
or send an email to specialmarkets@workman.com.

Workman Publishing Company, Inc.
225 Varick Street, New York, NY 10014-4381
workman.com

WORKMAN is a registered trademark of Workman Publishing Co., Inc.

Printed in the United States of America
First printing of new format August 2013

10 9 8 7 6 5 4 3 2 1

ABOUT THIS BOOK

The Little Book of Prayers is an anthology of prayers from around the world. Some prayers will be familiar, many not. The book is not intended to be comprehensive. Prayers are arranged in mood from "light" to "dark" or morning to night, and also by the serendipity of choice. An index and a selective guide are provided in the back to help the reader locate prayers by author and tradition, and by theme, occasion, or need.

INTRODUCTION

Prayer oneth the soul to God.

—JULIAN OF NORWICH

*H*ow soon after humans stood upright and turned
to the sky did they begin to pray? When did the
first person watch the sun rise and lift his heart in
praise? Or stand over a sick child and ask "Why?"
It must have been immediate; prayer seems almost as
natural as breathing. In editing a collection of prayers,
this is the first thing one understands—prayer, like
music or poetry, is everywhere in the world. Its
impulse is universal. And whether it is the Christian's
"Our Father" or a Navajo chant to the Lord of the
Mountains, the truths expressed in this impulse are
universal, too.

We pray to give thanks. We pray to ask for
answers. We pray to receive, pray to give. We very
much pray for help. We pray before we eat. And
before we sleep we ask "the Lord our souls to keep,"
to paraphrase the 12th-century prayer known by so

many Western children. There are names for different types of prayer—praise, petition, thanksgiving, and atonement are some. But we don't need to understand the terms to understand the soul's cry, or the beautiful language crafted to express it.

There is another universal quality to prayer, and that is humility. The Muslim surrenders. The Christian mystic prays to fold herself into the Lord. "Bow, stubborn knees!" says Hamlet. Even Jesus prayed, "Not what I will, but what thou wilt." Whether our prayer is to a God, a godhead, a spirit, or a tree, we can approach, literally or figuratively, only on our knees. Ego and arrogance have no place in prayer.

And in an age that could be characterized by its astonishing lack of humility, prayer offers a rare chance to put our inflated selves aside, and in the suddenly unburdened state that follows, rediscover the things that really matter. Which is perhaps why, living in the age that we do, we are also just beginning to rediscover the need for prayer.

*A*rise, you little glancing wings
    & sing your infant joy!
Arise & drink your bliss!
For every thing that lives is holy;
    for the source of life
Descends to be a weeping babe;
For the Earthworm renews the
    moisture of the sandy plain.

—WILLIAM BLAKE
"Vala, or The Four Zoas"

$\mathcal{T}$he light of God surrounds me;
The love of God enfolds me;
The power of God protects me;
The presence of God watches
    over me.
Wherever I am, God is.

—JAMES DILLET FREEMAN
"Prayer of Protection"

$\mathcal{I}$ shall sing a praise to God:
Strike the chords upon the drum.
God who gives us all good things—
Strike the chords upon the drum—
Wives, and wealth, and wisdom.
Strike the chords upon the drum.

—PRAYER FROM ZAIRE

*P*raise ye the LORD. Praise ye the LORD
from the heavens: praise him in the
heights.

Praise ye him, all his angels: praise ye him,
all his hosts.

Praise ye him, sun and moon: praise him,
all ye stars of light.

Praise him, ye heavens of heavens, and
ye waters that be above the heavens.

Let them praise the name of the LORD: for
he commanded, and they were created.

He hath also stablished them for ever and
ever: he hath made a decree which shall
not pass.

Praise the LORD from the earth, ye
dragons, and all deeps:

Fire, and hail; snow, and vapours;
stormy wind fulfilling his word:

Mountains, and all hills; fruitful trees,
   and all cedars;
Beasts, and all cattle; creeping things,
   and flying fowl:
Kings of the earth, and all people; princes,
   and all judges of the earth:
Both young men, and maidens; old men,
   and children:
Let them praise the name of the LORD:
   for his name alone is excellent; his glory
      is above the earth and heaven.
He also exalteth the horn of his people,
   the praise of all his saints; even of the
      children of Israel, a people near unto
         him. Praise ye the LORD.

—PSALM 148

We will sing thy praises,
O God almighty. We will now
and evermore sing thy praises,
even as they were sung of old.
For thy laws are immutable,
O God: they are firm like the
mountains.

— THE VEDAS

$\mathcal{Y}$ou are the notes, and we are the flute.
  We are the mountain, you are the sounds
    coming down.
  We are the pawns and kings and rooks
  you set out on a board: we win or we lose.
  We are lions rolling and unrolling on flags.
  Your invisible wind carries us through the
    world.

—JELALUDDIN RUMI

The earth has been laid down, the earth has
been laid down
The earth has been laid down, it has been
made,
The earth spirit has been laid down
It is covered over with growing things,
it has been laid down.
The earth has been laid down, it has been
made.
The sky has been set up, the sky has been
set up
The sky has been set up, it has been made.

The mountains have been laid down,
    the mountains have been laid down
The mountains have been laid down,
    they have been made.
The waters have been laid down, the waters
    have been laid down
The waters have been laid down, they have
    been made.
The clouds have been set up, the clouds
    have been set up
The clouds have been set up, they have
    been made.

—NAVAJO SWEATHOUSE CHANT

*W*herever I go—only Thou!
Wherever I stand—only Thou!
Just Thou, again Thou! always
Thou! Thou, Thou, Thou! When
things are good, Thou! when
things are bad—Thou! Thou,
Thou, Thou!

—HASIDIC SONG

The prayer preceding all prayers is "May it be the real I who speaks. May it be the real Thou that I speak to."

–C. S. Lewis

*B*lessed art Thou, Lord our God, King of
the universe, who forms light and creates
darkness, who makes peace and creates
all things.
Who mercifully sheds light upon the earth
and upon all who dwell on it.
And who in His goodness, renews the
works of creation every day continually.
"How many are Thy works O Lord,
in wisdom hast Thou made them all,
the earth is filled with Thy creations!"
Blessed art Thou, Lord our God, King of
the universe, who with His word brings
on the evenings,
With wisdom opens the gates,
With understanding alters the phases,
varies the seasons,

And arranges the stars in their heavenly
orbit according to His will.

He creates day and night.

He rolls away the light from before the
darkness and the darkness from before
the light,

He makes the day to pass and the night to
come, and divides between day and
night;

Lord of hosts in His name.

A living and everlasting God, who shall
constantly reign over us forever and
ever.

Blessed art Thou, Lord, who brings on
the evenings.

—JEWISH EVENING BLESSING
"Birkat Maariv"

In the Name of God, the merciful Lord
    of mercy.
Praise be to God, the Lord of all being,
the merciful Lord of mercy,
Master of the day of judgment.
You alone we serve: to You alone we come
    for aid.
Guide us in the straight path,
the path of those whom You have blessed,
not of those against whom there is
    displeasure,
nor of those who go astray.

—THE KORAN
"Opener Prayer"

$\mathcal{B}$e a gardener.
Dig a ditch,
toil and sweat,
and turn the earth upside down
and seek the deepness
and water the plants in time.
Continue this labor
and make sweet floods to run
and noble and abundant fruits to spring.
Take this food and drink
and carry it to God
as your true worship.

—JULIAN OF NORWICH

All you big things, bless the Lord
  Mount Kilimanjaro and Lake Victoria
  The Rift Valley and the Serengeti Plain
  Fat baobabs and shady mango trees
  All eucalyptus and tamarind trees
  Bless the Lord
  Praise and extol Him for ever and ever
  All you tiny things, bless the Lord

Busy black ants and hopping fleas

Wriggling tadpoles and mosquito larvae

Flying locusts and water drops

Pollen dust and tsetse flies

Millet seeds and dried dagaa

Bless the Lord

Praise and extol Him for ever and ever.

—East African Canticle

I believe a leaf of grass is no less
than the journey-work of the
stars,
And the pismire is equally perfect,
and a grain of sand, and the egg
of the wren,
And the tree-toad is a chef-
d'oeuvre for the highest,
And the running blackberry would
adorn the parlors of heaven,

And the narrowest hinge in my
    hand puts to scorn all
        machinery,
And the cow crunching with
    depress'd head surpasses any
        statue,
And a mouse is miracle enough to
    stagger sextillions of infidels.

—WALT WHITMAN

Make a joyful noise unto the LORD,
    all ye lands.
Serve the LORD with gladness: come before
    his presence with singing.
Know ye that the LORD he is God: it is he
    that hath made us, and not we ourselves;
        we are his people, and the sheep of his
            pasture.
Enter into his gates with thanksgiving, and
    into his courts with praise: be thankful
        unto him, and bless his name.
For the LORD is good; his mercy is
    everlasting; and his truth endureth to
        all generations.

—PSALM 100

With your feet I walk
I walk with your limbs
I carry forth your body
For me your mind thinks
Your voice speaks for me
Beauty is before me
And beauty is behind me
Above and below me hovers the beautiful
I am surrounded by it
I am immersed in it
In my youth I am aware of it
And in old age I shall walk quietly
The beautiful trail.

— NAVAJO PRAYER

The lark's on the wing;
The snail's on the thorn:
God's in his Heaven—
All's right with the world!

—ROBERT BROWNING

*B*less Thee, O Lord, for the living arc of
the sky over me this morning.

Bless Thee, O Lord, for the companionship
of night mist far above the skyscraper
peaks I saw when I woke once during
the night.

Bless Thee, O Lord, for the miracle of
light to my eyes and the mystery of it
ever changing.

Bless Thee, O Lord, for the laws Thou
hast ordained holding fast these tall
oblongs of stone and steel, holding fast
the planet Earth in its course and farther
beyond the cycle of the Sun.

—CARL SANDBURG

All Creation rejoices in you,
O Full of Grace,
The archangels and the race of men,
O Sanctified Temple and Spiritual
Paradise, the Glory of Virgins;
From whom God was incarnate
and became a child, our God
throughout the ages.
He made your body into a throne.
And your womb he made more
spacious than the heavens.
All creation rejoices in you,
O Full of Grace, glory to you!

—EASTERN ORTHODOX LITURGY

$\mathcal{M}$y praise dispraises
Thee, Almighty God,
For praise is being and to
be is sin.

—SUFI PRAYER

*M*y God, I love you.

—St. Thérèse of Lisieux
on Her Deathbed

Prayer is man's conversation with
God. It is the most secret and intimate
relationship which man can enter into with
the Lord of the Universe. He speaks with
God as 'thou' from a sense of innermost
closeness and tells Him everything which
troubles, moves and makes him happy. His
prayer may be improvised or he may use
an age-old form, a cliché sanctified by a
hundred generations and which has become
meaningful for man. He may say his prayer
aloud, chant it, whisper it or keep it in the
recesses of his heart.

— VLADIMIR LINDENBERG

$\mathcal{K}$eep me as the apple of
the eye,
hide me under the shadow
of thy wings.

—PSALM 17:8

$\mathcal{Y}$ou, O eternal Trinity, are a deep
sea into which, the more I enter,
the more I find, and the more I
find, the more I seek.
  O abyss,
    O eternal Godhead,
      O sea profound,
what more could you give me than
yourself?
Amen.

—St. Catherine of Siena

Lord, you are my lover,
My longing,
My flowing stream,
My sun,
And I am your reflection.

—MECHTHILD OF MAGDEBURG

O nectar! O delicious stream!
O ravishing and only pleasure!
　　Where Shall such another theme
Inspire my tongue with joys, or please
　　mine ear! Abridgment of delights!
　　　　And queen of sights!
O mine of rarities! O kingdom wide!
O more! O cause of all! O glorious bride!
　　O God! O bride of God! O king!
　　O soul and crown of everything!

　　　　　　　　　　—THOMAS TRAHERNE

*B*less the Lord, sun and moon, sing praise to him and highly exalt him for ever.

Bless the Lord, stars of heaven.

Bless the Lord, all rain and dew.

Bless the Lord, all winds.

Bless the Lord, fire and heat.

Bless the Lord, winter cold and summer heat.

Bless the Lord, dews and snows.

Bless the Lord, nights and days.

Bless the Lord, light and darkness.

Bless the Lord, ice and cold.

Bless the Lord, frosts and snows.

Bless the Lord, lightnings and clouds.

Let the earth bless the Lord; let it sing
praise to him and highly exalt him for ever.
Bless the Lord, mountains and hills.
Bless the Lord, all things that grow on
    the earth.
Bless the Lord, you springs.
Bless the Lord, seas and rivers.
Bless the Lord, you whales and all
    creatures that move in the waters.
Bless the Lord, all birds of the air.
Bless the Lord, all beasts and cattle,
    sing praise to him and highly exalt him
        for ever.

—SONG OF THE THREE YOUNG MEN

Lord, we brought in the harvest. The rain watered the earth, the sun drew cassava and corn out of the clay. Your mercy showered blessing after blessing over our country. Creeks grew into rivers; swamps became lakes. Healthy fat cows gaze on the green sea of the savanna. The rain smoothed out the clay walls, the mosquitoes drowned in the high waters.

Lord, the yam is fat like meat,
   the cassava melts on the tongue, oranges
   burst in their peels, dazzling and bright.

Lord, nature gives thanks,
   Your creatures give thanks. Your praise
   rises in us like the great river.

— WEST AFRICAN PRAYER

*P*raise God, from whom all
blessings flow!
Praise Him, all creatures here
below!
Praise Him above, ye heavenly
host!
Praise Father, Son, and
Holy Ghost!

—THOMAS KEN

$\mathcal{F}$or your sake I said I will praise the moon,
tell the colour of the river,
find new words for the agony
and ecstasy of gulls.

Because you are close,
everything that men make, observe
or plant is close, is mine:
the gulls slowly writhing, slowly singing
on the spears of wind;
the iron gate above the river;
the bridge holding between stone fingers
her cold bright necklace of pearls.

—LEONARD COHEN
"Owning Everything"

We praise Thee, O God, for Thy glory
displayed in all the creatures of the earth.
They affirm Thee in living; all things affirm
Thee in living; the bird in the air, both
the hawk and the finch; the beast on
the earth, both the wolf and the lamb; the
worm in the soil and the worm
in the belly.
Therefore man, whom Thou hast made to
be conscious of Thee, must consciously
praise Thee, in thought and in word and
in deed.

Even with the hand to the broom, the back
  bent in laying the fire, the knee bent in
  cleaning the hearth, we, the scrubbers
  and sweepers of Canterbury,
The back bent under toil, the knee bent
  under sin, the hands to the face under
  fear, the head bent under grief,
Even in us the voices of seasons, the snuffle
  of winter, the song of spring, the drone
  of summer, the voices of beasts and of
  birds, praise Thee.

–T. S. ELIOT
Murder in The Cathedral

*H*ow wonderful, O Lord, are the works
   of your hands!
The heavens declare Your glory,
   the arch of sky displays Your handiwork.
In Your love You have given us the power
   to behold the beauty of Your world
   robed in all its splendor.
The sun and the stars, the valleys and hills,
   the rivers and lakes all disclose Your
   presence.

The roaring breakers of the sea tell of
    Your awesome might;
the beasts of the field and the birds of the air
    bespeak Your wondrous will.
In Your goodness You have made us able
    to hear the music of the world. The
    voices of loved ones reveal to us that
    You are in our midst.
A divine voice sings through all creation.

—ADAPTATION OF PSALM 104

*T*o him with trumpets and
   with flutes,
With cornets, clarions,
   and with lutes,
With harps, with organs,
   and with shawms,
With holy anthems and
   with psalms,
With voice of angels
   and of men,
Sing Alleluia: amen, amen.

—JOHN DAVIES

*P*rayer is
The world in tune,
A spirit-voice,
And vocal joys
Whose *echo* is heaven's
bliss.

—HENRY VAUGHAN

Father of night, Father of day,
Father, who taketh the darkness away,
Father, who teacheth the bird to fly,
Builder of rainbows up in the sky,
Father of loneliness and pain,
Father of love and Father of rain.

Father of day, Father of night,
Father of black, Father of white,
Father, who build the mountain so high,
Who shapeth the cloud up in the sky,
Father of time, Father of dreams,
Father, who turneth the rivers and streams.

Father of grain, Father of wheat,
Father of cold and Father of heat,
Father of air and Father of trees,
Who dwells in our hearts and our
    memories,
Father of minutes, Father of days,
Father of whom we most solemnly praise.

—BOB DYLAN
"Father of Night"

I am bending my knee,
In the eye of the Father who
    created me,
In the eye of the Son who
    purchased me,
In the eye of the Spirit who
    cleansed me,
In friendship and affection.

—CELTIC RUNE

$\mathcal{H}$ail, holy queen,
mother of mercy, our life, our sweetness,
    and our hope.
To thee do we cry, poor banished children
    of Eve.
To thee do we send up our sighs
Mourning and weeping in this vale of tears.
Turn then, most gracious advocate,
Thine eyes of mercy toward us,
And after this exile
Show us the blessed fruit of thy womb, Jesus.
O clement, O loving, o sweet Virgin Mary.

Pray for us, O Holy Mother of God,
That we may be made worthy of the
    promises of Christ.

—PRAYER TO MARY
"Salve Regina"

$\mathcal{P}$raise be to him who alone is to be praised. Praise him for his grace and favour. Praise him for his power and goodness. Praise him whose knowledge encompasses all things.

O God, grant me light in my heart and light in my tomb, light in my hearing and light in my seeing, light in my flesh, light in my blood and light in my bones.

Light before me, light behind me,
light to right of me, light to left
of me, light above me, light
beneath me.

O God, increase my light and give
me the greatest light of all. Of thy
mercy grant me light, O thou most
merciful.

—ABU HAMID AL-GHAZALI

Glory be to God for dappled things—
 For skies of couple-colour as a brinded cow;
  For rose-moles all in stipple upon
   trout that swim;
Fresh-firecoal chestnut falls; finches' wings;
 Landscape plotted and pieced—fold,
  fallow, and plough;
   And all trades, their gear and tackle
   and trim.
All things counter, original, spare, strange;
 Whatever is fickle, freckled (who
 knows how?)
  With swift, slow; sweet, sour;
   adazzle, dim;
He fathers-forth whose beauty is past change:
  Praise him.

—GERARD MANLEY HOPKINS
"Pied Beauty"

$\mathcal{H}$e who is in the sun, and in the fire and in the heart of man is ONE. He who knows this is one with the ONE.

— THE UPANISHADS

Our Father which art in heaven,

Hallowed be thy name.

Thy kingdom come. Thy will be done in
earth, as it is in heaven.

Give us this day our daily bread.

And forgive us our debts, as we forgive our
debtors.

And lead us not into temptation, but deliver
us from evil:

For thine is the kingdom, and the power,
and the glory, for ever.

Amen.

—MATTHEW 6:9–13

*T*he Our Father contains all possible
petitions; we cannot conceive of any prayer
not already contained in it. It is to prayer
what Christ is to humanity. It is impossible
to say once through, giving the fullest
possible attention to each word, without
a change, infinitesimal perhaps but real,
taking place in the soul.

—SIMONE WEIL

O God, O lord of the mountains and valleys, I have offered you a bit of your food, your drink. And now I continue on, beneath your feet and your hands, I, a traveler.

Now I will sleep beneath your feet, beneath your hands, O lord of the mountains and valleys, O lord of the trees, O lord of the creeping vines. Again tomorrow there will be day, again tomorrow there will be light. I know not where I will be.

Who is my mother? Who is my father?
Only you, O God. You watch me, guard
me, on every path, through every darkness,
and before each obstacle that you might
hide or take away, O God, my lord, O lord
of the mountains and valleys.

—KEKCHI MAYA

We rose before dawn
to praise you,
bringing our song to your
   Lotus Feet—
hear what we ask!
Please listen,
you who were born among us
into this cowherding clan—
What choice do you have
but to take us into your service,
your heartfelt servants, your kin?

We didn't come to receive the
    outer drum,
the drum of a day, O Govinda—
We are yours for life.
Make all our desires be for you,
it is you alone that we want.
    Hear our song!

—ANTAL

My heart lies before you,
O my God. Look deep within.
See these memories of mine, for
you are my hope. You cleanse me
when unclean humours such as
these possess me, by drawing my
eyes to yourself and saving
my feet from the snare.

—St. Augustine

Oh my Lord,

If I worship you
from the fear of hell, burn me in hell.

If I worship you
from the hope of Paradise, bar me from
  its gates.

But if I worship you
for yourself alone, grant me the beauty
  of your Face.

—RABI'A

*W*hy should I call Thee Lord,
  Who art my God?
Why should I call Thee Friend,
  Who art my Love?
  Or King, Who art my very
    Spouse above?
Or call Thy Sceptre on my heart Thy rod?
  Lo now Thy banner over me is love,
All heaven flies open to me at Thy nod:
For Thou hast lit Thy flame in me a clod,
  Made me a nest for dwelling of Thy
    Dove.
  What wilt Thou call me in our home
    above,

Who now has called me friend?

    how will it be

  When Thou for good wine settest forth

    the best?

Now Thou dost bid me come and sup with

  Thee,

  Now Thou dost make me lean upon

    Thy breast:

  How will it be with me in time of Love?

—CHRISTINA ROSSETTI
"After Communion"

$\mathcal{T}$his world,
   compared to You—

a lake so tiny
   even a mustard seed
   is too large for it to hold.

Yet from the lake all Beings drink.

And into it deer, jackals,
    rhinoceri, sea-elephants falling.

From the earliest moment of birth,
    falling and falling in You.

—LAL DED

I find you, Lord, in all Things
 and in all
my fellow creatures, pulsing with
 your life;
as a tiny seed you sleep in what is
 small
and in the vast you vastly yield
 yourself.

—RAINER MARIA RILKE
The Book of Hours

*W*hen I am liberated by silence, when I am no longer involved in the measurement of life, but in the living of it, I can discover a form of prayer in which there is effectively no distraction. My whole life becomes a prayer. My whole silence is full of prayer. The world of silence in which I am immersed contributes to my prayer.

—THOMAS MERTON

Glorious Lord, I give you greeting!
Let the church and the chancel praise you.
Let the chancel and the church praise you.
Let the plain and the hillside praise you.
Let the world's three well-springs praise
    you.
Two above wind and one above land,
Let the dark and the daylight praise you.
Abraham, founder of the faith, praised you:
Let the life everlasting praise you.
Let the birds and honeybees praise you,
Let the shorn stems and the shoots praise
    you.
Both Aaron and Moses praised you:
Let the male and the female praise you,
Let the seven days and the stars praise you,

Let the air and the ether praise you,
Let the books and the letters praise you,
Let the fish in the swift streams praise you,
Let the thought and the action praise you,
Let the sand-grains and the earth-clods
   praise you,
Let all the good that's performed praise
   you.
And I shall praise you, Lord of glory:
Glorious Lord, I give you greeting!

—GAELIC BENEDICTION

*I*t is lovely indeed, it is lovely indeed.
I, I am the spirit within the earth . . .
The feet of the earth are my feet . . .
The legs of the earth are my legs . . .
The bodily strength of the earth is my
    strength . . .
The thoughts of the earth are my
    thoughts . . .
The voice of the earth is my voice . . .
The feather of the earth is my feather . . .
All that belongs to the earth belongs to
    me . . .
All that surrounds the earth surrounds
    me . . .
I, I am the sacred words of the earth . . .
It is lovely indeed, it is lovely indeed.

—NAVAJO SONG

*H*eaven is His head
Earth His feet.
Four compass points are His
   hands.
Sun and moon are His eyes.
Ether is His breath.
Fire is His mouth.
Teaching is His breast.
Non-teaching is His back.
Grass and plants are His hair.
Mountains are His bones.
Sea is His bladder.
Rivers are His veins.

—LAURETANIAN LITANY

I will be truthful.

I will suffer no injustice.

I will be free from fear.

I will not use force.

I will be of good will to
   all men.

—Mahatma Gandhi

Christ with me, Christ before me,
   Christ behind me,
Christ in me, Christ beneath me,
   Christ above me,
Christ on my right, Christ on my left,
Christ when I lie down, Christ when I
   sit down, Christ when I arise,
Christ in the heart of everyone who thinks
   of me,
Christ in the mouth of everyone who speaks
   of me,
Christ in every eye that sees me,
Christ in every ear that hears me.

—ST. PATRICK

It is right, O God, that peoples sing thy praises, and that they are glad and rejoice in thee. All evil spirits fly away in fear; but the hosts of the saints bow down before thee.

How could they not bow down in love and adoration, before thee, God of gods, Spirit Supreme? Thou creator of Brahma, the god of creation, thou infinite, eternal, refuge of the world! Thou who art all that is, and all that is not, and all that is Beyond.

Thou God from the beginning, God in man since man was. Thou Treasure supreme of this vast universe. Thou the One to be known and the Knower, the final resting place. Thou Infinite Presence in whom all things are.

Adoration unto thee who art before me and behind me: adoration unto thee who art on all sides, God of all. All-powerful God of immeasurable might. Thou art the consummation of all: thou art all.

—THE BHAGAVAD GITA

Glory to you for the feast-day of life.

Glory to you for the perfume of lilies
and roses.

Glory to you for each different taste of
berry and fruit.

Glory to you for the sparkling silver of
early morning dew.

Glory to you for the joy of dawn's
awakening.

Glory to you for the new life each day
brings.

— GREGORY PETROV

$\mathcal{W}$aking up this morning, I smile.
Twenty-four brand new hours are
    before me.
I vow to live fully in each moment
    and to look at all beings with
    eyes of compassion.

—THICH NHAT HANH

*T*herefore the limbs You have planted
   in us,
The spirit You have infused within us,
The tongue You have put in our mouths—
They shall all thankfully acknowledge,
   bless, praise, laud, exalt,
   glorify, sanctify, and proclaim Your
   sovereignty, O our king.
For every mouth shall acknowledge You,
Every tongue shall pledge loyalty to You,
Every knee shall bend to You,
Every back shall bow to You,
Every heart shall revere You,
Every inward part shall sing unto Your
   name—

As it is written:

  All my bones shall say,

    "Lord, who is like You?

    You save the poor from one stronger

      than he, the poor

    and needy from his despoiler"

      (Ps. 35:10).

—Sabbath Morning Prayer

$\mathcal{M}$y life is an instant,
a fleeting hour.
My life is a moment,
which swiftly escapes me.
O my God, you know that
on earth I have only today
to love you.

—St. Thérèse of Lisieux

Sometimes there is an expression of an almost physical longing to experience the presence of God, without whom life seems to have little meaning: "God, You are my God; I search for You, my soul thirsts for You, my body yearns for You" (Ps. 63:2).

—Reuven Hammer

Unbreakable, O Lord,
Is the love
That binds me to You:
Like a diamond,
It breaks the hammer that strikes it.

My heart goes into You
As the polish goes into the gold.
As the lotus lives in its water,
I live in You.

Like the bird
That gazes all night
At the passing moon,
I have lost myself dwelling in You.

O my Beloved—
Return.

—MIRABAI

I pray not for wealth,
I pray not for honours, I
pray not for pleasures, or
even the joys of poetry.
I only pray that during all
my life I may have love:
that I may have pure love
to love Thee.

—CHAITANYA

O love, O pure deep love,
   be here, be now
Be all; worlds dissolve into your
   stainless endless radiance,
Frail living leaves burn with you
   brighter than cold stars:
Make me your servant, your
   breath, your core.

—JELALUDDIN RUMI

love is not concerned
with whom you pray
or where you slept
the night you ran away
from home
love is concerned
that the beauty of your heart
should kill no one.

—ALICE WALKER
"Love Is Not Concerned"

God help us to live slowly:

To move simply:

To look softly:

To allow emptiness:

To let the heart create

   for us.

Amen.

—MICHAEL LEUNIG

O world, I cannot hold thee close enough!
　　Thy winds, thy wide grey skies!
　　Thy mists, that roll and rise!
Thy woods, this autumn day, that ache
　　and sag
And all but cry with colour! That gaunt crag
To crush! To lift the lean of that black bluff!
World, World, I cannot get thee close
　　enough!

Long have I known a glory in it all,

    But never knew I this:

    Here such a passion is

As stretcheth me apart,—Lord, I do fear

Thou'st made the world too beautiful

    this year;

My soul is all but out of me,—let fall

No burning leaf; prithee, let no bird call.

—EDNA ST. VINCENT MILLAY
"God's World"

$\mathcal{M}$y Joy—

My Hunger—

My Shelter—

My Friend—

My Food for the Journey—

My Journey's End—

You are my breath,

My hope,

My companion,

My craving,

My abundant wealth.

Without You—my Life, my Love—

I would never have wandered across these
endless countries.

You have poured out so much grace for me,
Done me so many favors, given me so
    many gifts—
I look everywhere for Your love—
Then suddenly I am filled with it.
O Captain of my Heart,
Radiant Eye of Yearning in my breast,
I will never be free from You
As long as I live.
Be satisfied with me, Love
And I am satisfied.

—RABI'A

*W*ouldest thou wit thy Lord's
meaning in this thing? Wit it well:
Love was his meaning.
Who shewed it thee? Love.
What shewed He thee? Love.
Wherefore shewed it He? for Love
. . . Thus was I learned that Love
is our Lord's meaning.

—JULIAN OF NORWICH

$\mathcal{M}$y soul doth magnify the Lord,
   And my spirit hath rejoiced in God my
      Saviour.
   For he that is mighty hath done to me great
      things; and holy is his name.
   And his mercy is on them that fear him
      from generation to generation.
   He hath shewed strength with his arm;
      he hath scattered the proud in the
         imagination of their hearts.
   He hath put down the mighty from their
      seats, and exalted them of low degree.
   He hath filled the hungry with good things;
      and the rich he hath sent empty away.

-Luke 1:46b-47, 49-53

I am thirsting for your love, my Beloved!

I shall make this body a lamp, and my
tender heart shall be its wick,

I shall fill it with the scented oil of my
young love and burn it night and day at
Your shrine, O Beloved!

For Your love I shall sacrifice all the wealth
of my youth;

Your name shall be the crown of my head.

I am longing for You, O my Lord: for the
season of the sowing has come;
but You are not beside me.

Clouds gather on my brows and my eyes
  shed heavy showers.
My parents gave me to You, I have become
  Yours for ever; who but You
    can be my Lord?
This separation troubles my breast; make
  me Your own; make me perfect
    like You, O Lord of Perfection!

— MIRABAI

$\mathcal{M}$ay the words of my
mouth and the meditation
of my heart be acceptable
to Thee, O Lord,
my Strength and my
Redeemer.

—JEWISH PRAYER
Conclusion of the "Shemoneh Esrei"

*P*rayer is in its essence the union of the
soul with God. Its effects and fruits are:
a pure soul, collection of inner forces,
reconciliation with God, tears, forgiveness
of sins, a bridge which leads us above
and over temptation, a wall of protection
against sorrows. It is the work of angels,
a food for all spiritual beings, the joy
of eternity, a divine action, a source of
virtues, a treasury of graces; it is spiritual
progress, the food of the soul, revelation,
the exclusion of faintheartedness, a prop for
our confidence, a comfort in grief.

—St. John Climacus

I asked for strength that I might achieve;
I was made weak that I might learn humbly
    to obey.
I asked for health that I might do greater
    things;
I was given infirmity that I might do better
    things.

I asked for riches that I might be happy;
I was given poverty that I might be wise.

I asked for power that I might have the
    praise of men;
I was given weakness that I might feel
    the need of God.

I asked for all things that I might enjoy life;
I was given life that I might enjoy all things.

I got nothing that I had asked for,
    but everything that I had hoped for.
Almost despite myself my unspoken
    prayers were answered;
I am, among all men, most richly blessed.

—Prayer of an Unknown
Confederate Soldier

$\mathcal{M}$ake us worthy, Lord, to serve
our fellow men throughout the
world who live and die in poverty
and hunger. Give them through
our hands this day their daily
bread, and by our understanding
love, give peace and joy.

– MOTHER TERESA

O Hidden Life vibrant in every
atom;
O Hidden Light! shining in every
creature;
O Hidden Love! embracing all in
Oneness;
May each who feels himself as one
with Thee,
Know he is also one with every
other.

—ANNIE BESANT

$\mathcal{H}$oly Spirit,
   giving life to all life,
   moving all creatures,
   root of all things,
   washing them clean,
   wiping out their mistakes,
   healing their wounds,
   you are our true life,
   luminous, wonderful,
   awakening the heart
   from its ancient sleep.

—HILDEGARD OF BINGEN

In the beginning was God,
Today is God,
Tomorrow will be God.
Who can make an image of God?
He has no body.
He is the word which comes out
  of your mouth.
That word! It is no more,
It is past, and still it lives!
So is God.

— PYGMY PRAYER

From all blindness of heart, from pride,
vainglory, and hypocrisy;
from envy, hatred, and malice, and all
uncharitableness,
Good Lord, deliver us.

—THE BOOK OF COMMON PRAYER

$\mathcal{L}$ook to this day,
For it is life,
The very life of life.
In its brief course lie all
The realities and verities of existence,
The bliss of growth,
The splendor of action,
The glory of power—

For yesterday is but a dream,
And tomorrow is only a vision,
But today, well lived,
Makes every yesterday a dream of
    happiness
And every tomorrow a vision of hope.

—SANSKRIT PROVERB

$\mathcal{T}$he world is charged with the grandeur
   of God.
   It will flame out, like shining from
      shook foil;
   It gathers to a greatness, like the ooze
      of oil
Crushed. Why do men then now not reck
   his rod?
Generations have trod, have trod, have trod;
   And all is seared with trade; bleared,
      smeared with toil;
   And wears man's smudge and shares
      man's smell: the soil
Is bare now, nor can foot feel, being shod.

And for all this, nature is never spent;
  There lives the dearest freshness deep
    down things;
  And though the last lights off the black
    West went
  Oh, morning, at the brown brink
    eastward, springs—
Because the Holy Ghost over the bent
  World broods with warm breast and
    with ah! bright wings.

—GERARD MANLEY HOPKINS
"God's Grandeur"

Why should I feel discouraged?
Why should the shadows fall?
Why should my heart feel lonely
and long for heaven and home?
When Jesus is my portion
A constant friend is he.

His eye is on the sparrow
And I know he watches me.

I sing because I'm happy,
I sing because I'm free.

His eye is on the sparrow
And I know he watches me.

—AFRICAN-AMERICAN SPIRITUAL

Deep peace of the running
  wave to you,
Deep peace of the flowing
  air to you,
Deep peace of the quiet
  earth to you,
Deep peace of the shining
  stars to you,
Deep peace of the Son of Peace
  to you.
Amen.

— GAELIC BLESSING

The LORD is my shepherd; I shall not
   want.
He maketh me to lie down in green pastures:
   he leadeth me beside the still waters.
He restoreth my soul: he leadeth me in
   the paths of righteousness for his
   name's sake.
Yea, though I walk through the valley of
   the shadow of death, I will fear no evil:
   for thou art with me; thy rod and thy
   staff they comfort me.

Thou prepareset a table before me in the
　　presence of mine enemies: thou anointest
　　my head with oil; my cup runneth over.
Surely goodness and mercy shall follow me
　　all the days of my life: and I will dwell in
　　the house of the LORD for ever.

　　　　　　　　　　　　　　　　—PSALM 23

*L*et nothing disturb thee,
Nothing affright thee;
All things are passing;
God never changeth;
Patient endurance
Attaineth to all things;
Who God possesseth
In nothing is wanting;
Alone God sufficeth.

—St. Teresa of Avila

Said the Holy One to Israel, "I have told you that when you pray, you should do so in the synagogue in your city. If you cannot pray in the synagogue, pray in your field. If you cannot pray in your field, pray in your house. If you cannot pray in your house, pray on your bed. If you cannot pray on your bed, meditate in your heart."

—MIDRASH PSALMS 4:9

$\mathcal{H}$e prayeth best, who loveth best
All things both great and small;
For the dear God who loveth us,
He made and loveth all.

—Samuel Taylor Coleridge

O most merciful redeemer, friend,
  and brother,
  may we know Thee more clearly,
  love Thee more dearly,
  and follow Thee more nearly,
  day by day.
Amen.

— RICHARD OF CHICHESTER

I want to be saved . . . and I want to save.
  Amen.
I want to be set free . . . and I want to free.
  Amen.
I want to be born . . . and I want to give
  birth. Amen.
I want to hear . . . and I want to be heard.
Sweetness dances. I want to pipe; all of
  you dance. Amen.
I want to run away . . . and I want to stay.
  Amen.
I want to make you beautiful . . . and I
  want to be beautiful. Amen.
I want to join with you . . . and I want to
  be joined. Amen.

I have no house . . . and I have houses.
  Amen.
I have no ground . . . and I have ground.
  Amen.
I have no temple . . . and I have temples.
  Amen.
If you look at me . . . I will be a lamp.
  Amen.
If you see me . . . I will be a mirror. Amen.
If you knock on me . . . I will be a door.
  Amen.
If you are a traveler . . . I will be a road.
  Amen.

This is my dance . . . Answer me with
  dancing.

—THE ACTS OF JOHN

Chilly water, chilly water,
Hallelujah to that lamb.
I know that water is chilly and cold,
Hallelujah to that lamb.
But I have Jesus in my soul,
Hallelujah to that lamb.
Satan's just like a snake in the grass
Hallelujah to that lamb.
He's watching for to bite you as you pass
Hallelujah to that lamb.

—AFRICAN-AMERICAN SPIRITUAL

Christ has no body now on earth but
    yours;
yours are the only hands with which he can
    do his work,
yours are the only feet with which he can go
    about the world,
yours are the only eyes through which his
compassion can shine forth upon a troubled
    world.
Christ has no body on earth now but yours.

—St. Teresa of Avila

Love bade me welcome: yet my soul
      drew back,
   Guiltie of dust and sinne.
But quick-ey'd Love, observing me grow
   slack From my first entrance in,
Drew nearer to me, sweetly questioning
   If I lack'd any thing.

"A guest," I answer'd, "worthy to be
      here": Love said, "You shall be he."
"I the unkinde, ungratefull? Ah, my deare,
   I cannot look on thee."
Love took my hand, and smiling did reply,
   "Who made the eyes but I?"

"Truth Lord, but I have marr'd them:
        let my shame
    Go where it doth deserve."
"And know you not," sayes Love, "who
        bore the blame?"
    "My deare, then I will serve."
"You must sit down," sayes Love, "and
        taste my meat":
    So I did sit and eat.

— GEORGE HERBERT
"A Dialogue Between God and the Soul"

$\mathcal{L}$ooking down into my father's
dead face
for the last time
my mother said without
tears, without smiles
without regrets
but with civility
"Goodnight, Willie Lee, I'll see you
in the morning."
And it was then I knew that the healing
of all our wounds
is forgiveness
That permits a promise of our return
at the end.

—ALICE WALKER

*M*ay all beings have happiness, and the
    causes of happiness;
May all be free from sorrow, and the causes
    of sorrow;
May all never be separated from the sacred
    happiness which is sorrowless;
And may all live in equanimity, without too
    much attachment and too much aversion,
And live believing in the equality of all
    that lives.

                        —BUDDHIST PRAYER

$\mathcal{M}$ake me pure, Lord:

  Thou art holy:

Make me meek, Lord:

  Thou wert lowly.

—GERARD MANLEY HOPKINS

More things are wrought
by prayer than this world
dreams of.

—ALFRED, LORD TENNYSON

*B*lessed are the poor in spirit:

    for their's is the kingdom of heaven.

Blessed are they that mourn:

    for they shall be comforted.

Blessed are the meek:

    for they shall inherit the earth.

Blessed are they which do hunger

    and thirst after righteousness:

      for they shall be filled.

Blessed are the merciful:

    for they shall obtain mercy.

Blessed are the pure in heart:

    for they shall see God.

Blessed are the peacemakers:

    for they shall be called the children

        of God.

Blessed are they which are persecuted

    for righteousness' sake:

        for their's is the kingdom of heaven.

—MATTHEW 5:3–10

Sir spirit, forgive me my sins,
Sir spirit give me your blessing
  again,
Sir Spirit forgive my phantom
  body's demands,
Sir Spirit thanks for your kindness
  past. . . .

—ALLEN GINSBERG
"Elegy for Neal Cassady"

$\mathcal{B}$ecause between now and
tomorrow, maybe I, God, will
    have passed by your way . . .
Blessed is he who puts off, that is
    to say,
Blessed is he who hopes. And who
    sleeps.

—CHARLES PÉGUY

$\mathcal{M}$ay the power of God this day enable me,

    the nakedness of God disarm me,

    the beauty of God silence me,

    the justice of God give me voice,

    the integrity of God hold me,

    the desire of God move me,

    the fear of God expose me to the truth,

    the breath of God give me abundant life.

—JANET MORLEY

$\mathcal{L}$et our sleeping soul
remember, and be
awake and be alive, in
contemplation, of how our
life passes away, of how
our death comes forward
to us, so silently.

—JORGE MANRIQUE

*L*iving beings are without
number: I vow to row them
to the other shore.
Defilements are without number:
I vow to remove them from
myself.
The teachings are immeasurable:
I vow to study and practice
them.
The way is very long: I vow to
arrive at the end.

—FOUR VOWS OF THE BODDHISATTVA

Meditation, then, is
bringing the mind home.

—SOGYAL RINPOCHE

We were enclosed,
  O eternal Father,
  within the garden of your breast.
  You drew us out of your holy mind
    like a flower
  petaled with our soul's three
    powers,
  and into each power
  you put the whole plant,
  so that they might bear fruit in
    your garden,
  might come back to you
  with the fruit you gave them.

And you would come back to
    the soul,
to fill her with your blessedness.
There the soul dwells—
like the fish in the sea
and the sea in the fish.

—St. Catherine of Siena

$\mathcal{A}$s the bridegroom
rejoiceth over the bride,
so shall thy God rejoice
over thee.

—Isaiah 62:5

May the road rise up to meet you.
  May the wind be always at your back.
  May the sun shine warm upon your face,
  the rains fall soft upon your fields
  and until we meet again,
  may God hold you in the palm of His hand.

—GAELIC BLESSING

Cut through, O lord,
my heart's greed,
and show me
your way out.

O lord white as jasmine.

∞

After this body has known my lord
   who cares if it feeds
   a dog
   or soaks up water?

Like an elephant
lost from his herd
suddenly captured,

remembering his mountains,
   his Vindhyas,
   I remember.

O lord white as jasmine
   show me
   your ways.
      Call me: Child, come here,
      come this way.

— MAHADEVIYAKKA

King of Glorie, King of Peace,
   I will love thee;
And that love may never cease,
   I will move thee.

Thou hast granted my request,
   Thou hast heard me;
Thou didst note my working breast,
   Thou hast spar'd me.

Wherefore with my utmost art
 I will sing thee,
And the cream of all my heart
 I will bring thee.

∞

Small it is, in this poor sort
 To enrol thee:
E'en eternitie's too short
 To extol thee.

—GEORGE HERBERT

$\mathcal{T}$hou my mother, and my father
thou
Thou my friend, and my teacher
thou
Thou my wisdom, and my riches
thou
Thou art all to me, O God of all
Gods.

—RAMANUJA INDIAN PRAYER

Better than a hundred years lived in
ignorance, without contemplation, is
one single day of life lived in wisdom and
in deep contemplation.

Better than a hundred years lived in
idleness and in weakness is a single day
of life lived with courage and powerful
striving.

Better than a hundred years not considering
how all things arise and pass away is one
single day of life if one considers how all
things arise and pass away.

Better than a hundred years not seeing
one's own immortality is one single day
of life if one sees one's own immortality.

—THE DHAMMAPADA

$\mathcal{N}$ight is drawing nigh.
For all that has been—
Thanks!
For all that shall be—
Yes!

—DAG HAMMARSKJÖLD

*I*t is prayer that restores
to us the ability to feel, to
see, and to appreciate.

—REUVEN HAMMER

Rejoice evermore.

Pray without ceasing.

In every thing give thanks.

—1 Thessalonians 5:16–18

i thank You God for most this amazing
    amazing
day:for the leaping greenly spirits
    of trees
and a blue true dream of sky;and
    for everything
which is natural which is infinite
    which is yes

—E. E. CUMMINGS

We thankfully acknowledge You,
   O Lord our God,
for granting our ancestors the inheritance
   of a pleasant, good, and spacious land,
for taking us out of the land of Egypt, O
   Lord our God, and redeeming us from
   the house of bondage,
for the covenant which You have implanted
   in our flesh,
for the Torah which You have taught us,
for the laws which You have revealed to us,
for life, grace, and kindness which You
   have bestowed upon us,

and for the food with which You always
   provide us, every day, at all seasons and
   times.
For all this do we thankfully acknowledge
   You and bless You
—may Your name be continually blessed by
   all living beings forever and ever—
as it is written: When you have eaten your
   fill, bless the Lord your God for the
   good land which He has given you
   (Dt. 8:10).

—JEWISH MEALTIME BLESSING
"Birkat Ha-Mazon"

O my God,

the soul You have placed within me is pure.
You created it, You formed it, You breathed
it within me, You guard it within me, You
will take it from me in the future and will
restore it to me in the future-to-come.
As long as the soul is within me I thankfully
acknowledge You, O Lord my God and
God of my fathers, Master of all deeds,
Lord of all souls.
Blessed are You, O Lord, who restores
souls to the dead.

—THE TALMUD

O God, give me, I pray Thee,
light on my right hand
and light on my left hand
and light above me
and light beneath me,
O Lord, increase light within me
and give me light
and illuminate me.

—Ascribed to Muhammad

$\mathcal{L}$ike a golden beacon signaling
   on a moonless night,
Tao guides our passage through
   this transitory realm.
In moments of darkness and pain
remember all is cyclical.
Sit quietly behind; your wooden
   door:
Spring will come again.

—LOY CHING YUEN

I will extol thee, O LORD; for thou hast
   lifted me up, and hast not made my foes
   to rejoice over me.
O LORD my God, I cried unto thee, and
   thou hast healed me.
O LORD, thou hast brought up my soul
   from the grave: thou hast kept me alive,
   that I should not go down to the pit.
Sing unto the LORD, O ye saints of his,
   and give thanks at the remembrance of
   his holiness.
For his anger endureth but a moment;
   in his favour is life: weeping may endure
   for a night, but joy cometh in the
   morning.

                                     —PSALM 30:1–5

*E*arth our mother, breathe forth life
    all night sleeping
      now awaking
    in the east
    now see the dawn

Earth our mother, breathe and waken
    leaves are stirring
    all things moving
    new day coming
life renewing

                              —PAWNEE PRAYER

$\mathcal{B}$less
something small
but infinite
and quiet.

There are senses
make an object
in their simple
feeling for one.

—ROBERT CREELEY
"A Prayer"

We return thanks to our mother,
the earth, which sustains us.
We return thanks to the rivers and streams,
which supply us with water.
We return thanks to all herbs,
which furnish medicines for the cure to our
diseases.
We return thanks to the corn, and to her
sisters, the beans and squashes,
which give us life.
We return thanks to the bushes and trees,
which provide us with fruit.
We return thanks to the wind,
which, moving in the air, has banished
diseases.

We return thanks to the moon and stars,
    which have given to us their light
    when the sun was gone.
We return thanks to our grandfather Hé-no,
    that he has protected his grandchildren
    from witches and reptiles,
    and has given to us his rain.
We return thanks to the sun,
    that he has looked upon the earth
    with a beneficent eye.
Lastly, we return thanks to the Great Spirit,
    in whom is embodied all goodness,
    and who directs all things
    for the good of his children.

—IROQUOIS PRAYER

If He had fed us with manna,
and had not given us the Sabbath,
it would have sufficed.

If He had given us the Sabbath,
and had not brought us to
Mount Sinai,
it would have sufficed.

If He had brought us near to
Mount Sinai,
and had not given us the Law,
it would have sufficed.

If He had given us the Law,
and had not led us into the land
of Israel,
it would have sufficed.

If He had led us into the land
of Israel
and not built the temple,
it would have sufficed.

—JEWISH PRAYER FOR PASSOVER
"Dayanu"

Lord, I am grateful to You
that in Your mysterious love
You have taken away from me
all earthly wealth,
and that You now clothe and feed me
through the kindness of others.

Lord, I am grateful to You
that since You have taken away from me
the sight of my eyes.
You care for me now
through the eyes of others.

Lord, I am grateful to You
that since you have taken away from me
the strength of my hands and heart,
you care for me now
through the hands and hearts of others.

Lord, I pray for them,
that You will reward them in Your love,
that they may continue to faithfully serve
and care until they come to a happy end
in eternity with You.

— MECHTHILD OF MAGDEBURG

*T*his ritual is one.

The food is one.

We who offer the food are one.

The fire of hunger is also one.

All action is one.

We who understand this are one.

—Ancient Hindu Blessing

*P*rayer is for the soul,
what food is for the body.
The blessing of one prayer
lasts until the next, just as
the strength gained from
one meal lasts till the one
after.

—JEWISH PRAYER

Blessed are you,
O Lord Our God,
Eternal King, .

Who feeds the whole world
With your goodness, —
With grace, with loving kindness,
And with tender mercy.

You give food to all flesh,
For Your loving kindness endures forever.
Through Your great goodness,
Food has never failed us.
O may it not fail us forever;

For Your name's sake, since You
Nourish and sustain all living things
And do good to all,
And provide food for all Your creatures
Whom You have created.

Blessed are You, O Lord,
Who gives food to all.

—ANCIENT JEWISH BLESSING

$\mathcal{B}$e with me, O God, at breaking
of bread,
Be with me, O God, at the close
of my meal;
Let no whit adown my body
That may hurt my sorrowing soul.
O no whit adown my body
That may hurt my sorrowing soul.

—GAELIC GRACE

$\mathcal{T}$he bread is pure and
    fresh,
the water is cool and clear.
Lord of all life, be with us,
Lord of all life, be near.

—AFRICAN GRACE

O my brothers of the wilderness,
My little brothers,
For my necessities
I am about to kill you!
May the Master of Life who made you
In the form of the quarry
That the children may be fed,
Speedily provide you
Another house;
So there may be peace
Between me and thy spirit.

—MARY AUSTIN

$\mathcal{L}$ord, behold our family here assembled.
We thank you for this place in which we
dwell,
for the love that unites us,
for the peace accorded us this day,
for the hope with which we expect the
morrow;
for the health, the work, the food and
the bright skies
that make our lives delightful;
for our friends in all parts of the earth.
Amen.

—ROBERT LOUIS STEVENSON

Our father, hear us, and our
grandfather. I mention also
all those that shine, the
yellow day, the good wind,
the good timber, and the good earth.

All the animals, listen to me
under the ground. Animals
above ground, and water
animals, listen to me. We
shall eat your remnants of
food. Let them be good.

Let there be long breath and life.

    Let the people increase, the

    children of all ages, the girls

    and the boys, and the men

    of all ages and the women,

    the old men of all ages and

    the old women. The food

    will give us strength

    whenever

    the sun runs.

Listen to us, Father, Grandfather.

    We ask thought, heart,

    love, happiness. We are

    going to eat.

—ARAPAHO PRAYER BEFORE EATING

$\mathcal{T}$he food which we are about to eat
Is Earth, Water and Sun, compounded
    through the alchemy of many plants.
Therefore Earth, Water and Sun will
    become part of us.
This food is also the fruit of the labor of
    many beings and creatures.
We are grateful for it.

May it give us strength, health, joy.

And may it increase our love.

—UNITARIAN PRAYER

We venerate the Three Treasures:
Buddha, Dharma, Sangha,
And are thankful for this meal,
The work of many people
And the sharing of other forms
   of life.

— ZEN PRAYER

$\mathcal{F}$irst, seventy-two labors brought us this
food,
We should know how it comes to us.
Second, as we receive this offering,
We should consider
Whether our virtue and practice deserve it.
Third, as we desire the natural order of
mind,
To be free from clinging,
We must be free from greed.
Fourth, to support our life, we take this
food.
Fifth, to attain our way we take this food.
First, this food is for the Three Treasures.
Second, it is for our teachers, parents,
nation,

And all sentient beings.

Third, it is for all beings in the three
worlds.

Thus, we eat this food with everyone,

We eat to stop all evil, to practice good,

To save all sentient beings,

And to accomplish our Buddha Way.

—MEAL GATHA

*L*et us not forget what Thou
hast done for us, and when Thy
helping hand hath wondrously
been there, then let us not seek
it again as ungrateful beings who
only ate and were satisfied.

—SØREN KIERKEGAARD

ABOUT PRAYER

*A*nd when thou prayest, thou shalt not
be as the hypocrites are: for they love to
pray standing in the synagogues and in the
corners of the streets, that they may be seen
of men. Verily I say unto you, They have
their reward.

But thou, when thou prayest, enter into
thy closet, and when thou hast shut thy
door, pray to thy Father which is in secret;
and thy Father which seeth in secret shall
reward thee openly.

—MATTHEW 6:5–6

*T*hat you may have pleasure in
 everything
Seek your own pleasure in
 nothing.
That you may know everything
Seek to know nothing.
That you may possess all things
Seek to possess nothing.
That you may be everything
Seek to be nothing.

—St. John of the Cross

$\mathcal{T}$is the gift to be simple,
'Tis the gift to be free,
'Tis the gift to come down
Where we ought to be—
And when we find ourselves
In the place just right,
'Twill be in the valley
Of love and delight.
When true simplicity is gained,
To bow and to bend
We shan't be asham'd,
To turn, turn will be our delight,
Till by turning, turning
We come round right.

—SHAKER HYMN

OM.
This eternal Word is all:
what was, what is and
what shall be, and what
beyond is in eternity. All is
OM.

—THE UPANISHADS

The fewer the words,
the better the prayer.

—MARTIN LUTHER

$\mathcal{M}$ay there be peace in the higher regions;
may there be peace in the firmament; may
there be peace on earth. May the waters
flow peacefully; may the herbs and plants
grow peacefully; may all the divine powers
bring unto us peace. The supreme Lord is
peace. May we all be in peace, peace, and
only peace; and may that peace come unto
each of us.

Shanti — Shanti — Shanti!
(Peace — Peace — Peace!)

—THE VEDAS

Come, my beloved, let
    us greet the bride, let us
    welcome Shabbos,
A peaceful and blessed
    Shabbos.

—S ABBATH P RAYER

O God, you have formed
heaven and earth;
You have given me all the
goods
that the earth bears!
Here is your part, my God.
Take it!

—PRAYER FROM ZAIRE

Grant me to recognize in other men, Lord God, the radiance of your own face.

— TEILHARD DE CHARDIN

If I spent enough time with the tiniest creature—
even a caterpillar—
I would never have to prepare a sermon. So full of God is every creature.

—MEISTER ECKHART

*H*ere I am at Your service,
   O Lord, here I am.
Here I am. No partner do You have.
   Here I am.
Truly, the praise and the favor is
   Yours, and the dominion.
No partner do You have.

—MUSLIM PRAYER
"Talbiyyah"

Late have I loved you, O beauty
so ancient and so new;
   late have I loved you.
You called and cried to me and
broke upon my deafness;
   and you sent forth your light
and shone upon me,
and chased away my blindness;

You breathed fragrance upon me,
    and I drew in my breath and do
not pant for you:
I tasted you and I now hunger and
thirst for you;
    you touched me, and I have
burned for your peace.

—St. Augustine

I pray Thee, O gracious Lord,
Grant that this mendicant may
  cling successfully to solitude,
Making solitude his paradise.

—BUDDHIST PRAYER

For prayer is a request.
The essence of request, as
distinct from compulsion,
is that it may or may not
be granted.

–C. S. Lewis

I want to want to want to want you God.

—Michael Ramsey

$\mathcal{Y}$ou, whose day it is,
make it beautiful. Get out
your rainbow colors, so it
will be beautiful.

—NOOTKA SONG

Lord, make me an instrument of your
    peace.
Where there is hatred, let me sow love,
Where there is injury, pardon;
Where there is doubt, faith;
Where there is despair, hope;
Where there is darkness, light;
And where there is sadness, joy.

O, Divine Master, grant that I may not
so much
seek to be consoled as to console,
to be understood as to understand,
to be loved, as to love.

For it is in giving that we receive,
it is in pardoning that we are
pardoned,
and it is in dying that we are born to
eternal life.

—St. Francis of Assisi

Spirit of the living God,
  fall afresh on us.
Spirit of the living God,
  fall afresh on us.
Melt us, mould us,
  fill us, use us.
Spirit of the living God,
  fall afresh on us.

—MICHAEL IVERSON

O Thou who art at home
Deep in my heart
Enable me to join you
Deep in my heart.

—THE TALMUD

Now this day,
My sun father,
Now that you have come out
standing to your sacred place,
That from which we draw the
water of life,
Prayer meal
Here I give you.

Your long life,
Your old age,
Your waters,
Your seeds,
Your riches,
Your power,
Your strong spirit,
All these to me may you grant.

—Zuñi Prayer at Sunrise

Oh Allah! I ask Thee for joyful patience, great reward; sincere turning; a remembering tongue; forbearing body; increased subsistence, beneficial knowledge and good action; granted supplication; forgiven sin; honest livelihood; decent children; wholesome cure; a blessed destination; a victory close at hand; and lasting bliss and the Paradise, and silk, and freshness and vigour, and delight, by Thy mercy, Oh Most Merciful of the Merciful!

—MUSLIM PRAYER
"Namaz-e-Isha"

I cannot dance, O Lord,
Unless You lead me.
If You wish me to leap joyfully,
Let me see You dance and sing—

Then I will leap into Love—
And from Love into Knowledge,
And from Knowledge into the Harvest,
That sweetest Fruit beyond human sense.

There I will stay with You, whirling.

—MECHTHILD OF MAGDEBURG

Come, Holy Spirit,
And send out from heaven
The beam of your light.

—ARCHBISHOP STEPHEN LANGTON
"The Golden Sequence," Whitsunday

Sun, my relative
Be good coming out
Do something good for us.

Make me work,
So I can do anything in the garden
I hoe, I plant corn, I irrigate.

You, sun, be good going down at sunset
We lay down to sleep I want to feel good.

While I sleep you come up.
Go on your course many times.
Make good things for us men.

Make me always the same as I am now.

—HAVASUPAI PRAYER

Here's the thing, say Shug. The thing I believe. God is inside you and inside everybody else. You come into the world with God. But only them that search for it inside find it. And sometimes it just manifest itself even if you not looking, or don't know what you looking for. Trouble do it for most folks, I think. Sorrow, lord. Feeling like shit.

It? I ast.

Yeah, It. God ain't a he or a she, but a It.

But what do it look like? I ast.

Don't look like nothing, she say. It ain't a picture show. It ain't something you can look at apart from anything else, including yourself. I believe God is everything, say Shug. Everything that is or ever was or ever will be. And when you can feel that, and be happy to feel that, you've found It.

Shug a beautiful something, let me tell you. She frown a little, look out cross the yard, lean back in her chair, look like a big rose.

She say, My first step from the old white man was trees. Then air. Then birds. Then other people. But one day when I was sitting quiet and feeling like a motherless child, which I was, it come to me: that feeling of being part of everything, not separate at all. I knew that if I cut a tree, my arm would bleed. And I laughed and I cried and I run all round the house. I knew just what it was. In fact, when it happen, you can't miss it.

—ALICE WALKER
The Color Purple

O our Father the Sky, hear us
   and make us bold.
O our Mother the Earth, hear us
   and give us support.
O Spirit of the East,
   send us your Wisdom.
O Spirit of the South,
   may we walk your path of life.
O Spirit of the West,
   may we always be ready for the long
   journey.
O Spirit of the North, purify us
   with your cleansing winds.

—SIOUX PRAYER

*S*ay your prayers in a melody that
is most pleasant and sweet to you.
Then you shall pray with proper
kavanah, because the melody will
draw your heart after the words
come from your mouth. Supplicate
in a melody that makes the heart
weep, praise in a melody that
makes the heart glad.

—Rabbi Hayim Halevy Donin

Lord of the springtime, Father of flower, field and fruit, smile on us in these earnest days when the work is heavy and the toil wearisome; lift up our hearts, O God, to the things worthwhile—sunshine and night, the dripping rain, the song of the birds, books and music, and the voices of our friends. Lift up our hearts to these this night and grant us Thy peace. Amen.

—W.E.B. DU BOIS

Come, true light.

Come, life eternal.

Come, hidden mystery.

Come, treasure without name.

Come, rejoicing without end.

Come, light that knows no evening.

Come, raising of the fallen.

Come, resurrection of the dead.

Come, for you are yourself the desire that is
within me.

Come, my breath and my life.

Come, the consolation of my humble soul.

Come, my joy, my glory, my endless delight.

—St. Symeon

Earth teach me stillness
   as the grasses are stilled with light.
Earth teach me suffering
   as old stones suffer with memory.
Earth teach me humility
   as blossoms are humble with beginning.
Earth teach me caring
   as the mother who secures her young.
Earth teach me courage
   as the tree which stands all alone.
Earth teach me limitation
   as the ant which crawls on the ground.

Earth teach me freedom
  as the eagle which soars in the sky.
Earth teach me resignation
  as the leaves which die in the fall.
Earth teach me regeneration
  as the seed which rises in the spring.
Earth teach me to forget myself
  as melted snow forgets its life.
Earth teach me to remember kindness
  as dry fields weep with rain.

—UTE PRAYER

Lord, I have loved Your sky,
Be it said against or for me,
Have loved it clear and high,
Or low and stormy;

Till I have reeled and stumbled
From looking up too much,
And fallen and been humbled
To wear a crutch.

My love for every Heaven
O'er which You, Lord, have lorded,
From number One to Seven,
Should be rewarded.

It may not give me hope
That when I am translated
My scalp will in the cope
Be constellated.

But if that seems to tend
To my undue renown,
At least it ought to send
Me up, not down.

—ROBERT FROST
"Astrometaphysical"

O heavenly Father, protect and bless all things that have breath: guard them from all evil and let them sleep in peace.

—ALBERT SCHWEITZER
"A Child's Prayer"

That our earth mother may wrap herself
In a fourfold robe of white meal;
That she may be covered with frost flowers;
That yonder on all the mossy mountains
The forests may huddle together with
   the cold;
That their arms may be broken by the
   snow,
in order that the land may be thus,
I have made my prayer sticks into living
   beings.

—ZUÑI OFFERING

The LORD bless thee,
and keep thee: The LORD
make his face shine upon
thee, and be gracious unto
thee: The LORD lift up his
countenance upon thee,
and give thee peace.

–NUMBERS 6:24–26

Come, Holy Spirit, fill the hearts
   of your faithful,
and enkindle in them the fire of
   your love.
Send forth your Spirit and they
   shall be created.
And you shall renew the face of
   the earth.
Let us pray.

—Attributed to Rabanus Maurus

O great God of Heaven,
Draw Thou my soul to Thyself
That I may make repentance
With a right and a strong heart,
With a heart broken and contrite,
That shall not change nor bend nor yield.

O great God of the angels,
Bring Thou me to the dwelling of peace;
O great God of the angels,
Preserve me from the evil of the fairies;
O great God of the angels,
Bathe me in the bathing of Thy pool.

—CELTIC PRAYER

$\mathcal{F}$ather in Heaven! Reawaken conscience in our breast. Make us bend the ear of the spirit to Thy voice, so that we may perceive Thy will for us in its clear purity as it is in Heaven, pure of our false worldly wisdom, unstifled by the voice of passion; keep us vigilant so that we may work for our salvation with fear and trembling; oh, but grant also that when the Law speaks most strongly, when its seriousness fills us with dread, when the thunder booms from Sinai—Oh grant that we may hear also a gentle voice murmuring to us that we are Thy children, so that we will cry with joy, Abba, Father.

—SØREN KIERKEGAARD

Jesus, will you come by here
  O Jesus, will you come by here
  Jesus will you come by here.
  Now is a needed time
  O now is a needed time
  Now is a needed time.

Come if you don't stay long
O come if you don't stay long
Come if you don't stay long.
Now is a needed time
O now is a needed time
Now is a needed time.

Prayin' for you to come by here
I'm prayin' for you to come by here
Jesus won't you come by here, come by here.
Now is a needed time
Right now Lord is a needed time
Now is a needed time.

∞

Down on my knees an' prayin'
Down on my knees an' prayin'
Jesus won't you come by here.
Jesus won't you come by here
O Jesus won't you come by here
Jesus won't you come by here.

—LIGHTNIN' HOPKINS
"Needed Time"

May Heaven guard and keep you,
  Cause your grain to prosper,
  Send you nothing that is not good.
  May you receive from Heaven a
    hundred boons,
  May Heaven send down to you
    blessings so many
  That the day is not long enough
    for them all.

—THE BOOK OF SONGS
"Blessings on Gentle Folk"

In prayer,
come empty,
do nothing.

—St. John of the Cross

$\mathcal{T}$ake time to listen to what is said without words, to obey the law too subtle to be written, to worship the unnameable and to embrace the unformed.

—LAO-TZU

$\mathcal{F}$riend, if thou wilt be
    something, stand
    not still:
Thou must from one light
    to another go.

—ANGELUS SILESIUS

Ho! Sun, Moon, Stars, all that move in
the heavens
I bid you hear me!
Into your midst has come a new life.
Consent, I implore you!
Make its path smooth, that it may reach
the brow of the first hill!

Ho! You Winds, Clouds, Rain, Mist,
all you that move in the air,
I bid you hear me!
Into your midst has come a new life.
Consent, I implore you!
Make its path smooth, that it may reach
the brow of the second hill!

Give us, Lord, a humble, quiet, peaceable, patient, tender and charitable mind, and in all our thoughts, words and deeds a taste of the Holy Spirit. Give us, Lord, a lively faith, a firm hope, a fervent charity, a love of you. Take from us all lukewarmness in meditation, dullness in prayer. Give us fervour and delight in thinking of you and your grace, your tender compassion towards me. The things that we pray for, good Lord, give us grace to labour for: through Jesus Christ our Lord.

—ST. THOMAS MORE

The best help in all action is—to pray, that is true genius; then one never goes wrong.

—SØREN KIERKEGAARD

*L*et me seek you in my desire,
Let me desire you in my seeking.
Let me find you by loving you
Let me love you when I find you.

—ST. ANSELM

O our Mother the Earth, O our Father
   the Sky,
Your children are we, and with tired backs
We bring you the gifts you love.
Then weave for us a garment of brightness;
May the warp be the white light of morning,
May the weft be the red light of evening,
May the fringes be the falling rain,
May the border be the standing rainbow.
Thus weave for us a garment of brightness,
That we may walk fittingly where birds sing,
That we may walk fittingly where grass
   is green,
O our Mother the Earth, O our Father
   the Sky.

—TEWA PRAYER
"Song of the Sky Loom"

O Heavenly King, the Comforter, the Spirit of Truth who art everywhere and fillest all things. Treasury of Blessings, and Giver of Life: Come and abide in us, and cleanse us from every impurity, and save our souls, O Good One.

O most-holy Trinity: have mercy on us. O Lord: cleanse us from our sins. O Master: pardon our transgressions. O Holy One: visit and heal our infirmities, for Thy name's sake.

—ST. JOHN CHRYSOSTOM

$\mathcal{F}$orgive, O Lord, my little
jokes on Thee
And I'll forgive Thy great
big one on me.

—ROBERT FROST
In the Clearing

$\mathcal{M}$y period had come for Prayer—
  No other Art—would do—
  My Tactics missed a rudiment—
  Creator—Was it you?

  God grows above—so those who pray
  Horizons—must ascend—
  And so I stepped upon the North
  To see this Curious Friend—

  His House was not—no sign had He—
  By Chimney—nor by Door
  Could I infer his Residence—
  Vast Prairies of Air

Unbroken by a Settler—
Were all that I could see—
Infinitude—Had'st Thou no Face
That I might look on Thee?

The Silence condescended—
Creation stopped—for Me—
But awed beyond my errand—
I worshipped—did not "pray"—

—Emily Dickinson

*J*esus, lover of my soul,
  Let me to Thy bosom fly,
  While the waters nearer roll,
  While the tempest still is high;
  Hide me, O my Savior, hide,
  Till the storm of life is past;
  Safe into the haven glide,
  O receive my soul at last.

—CHARLES WESLEY
"Jesus, Lover of My Soul"

*L*ord Jesus Christ, pierce my soul with your love so that I may always long for you alone, who are the bread of angels and the fulfillment of the soul's deepest desires. . . . May my soul thirst for you, who are the source of life, wisdom, knowledge, light and all the riches of God our Father. May I always seek and find you, think upon you, speak to you and do all things for the honour and glory of your holy name. Be always my only hope, my peace, my refuge and my help in whom my heart is rooted so that I may never be separated from you.

—ST. BONAVENTURE

O Lord, grant me to greet the coming day in peace. Help me in all things to rely upon thy holy will. In every hour of the day reveal thy will to me. Bless my dealings with all who surround me. Teach me to treat all that comes to me throughout the day with peace of soul, and with firm conviction that thy will governs all. In all my deeds and words guide my thoughts and feelings. In unforeseen events let me not forget that all are sent by thee. Teach me to act firmly and wisely, without embittering and embarrassing others. Give me strength to bear the fatigue of the coming day with all that it shall bring. Direct my will, teach me to pray, pray thou thyself in me. Amen.

—EASTERN ORTHODOX PRAYER

O abyss, O Eternal Godhead, O sea profound, what more could you give me than yourself? You are the fire that ever burns without being consumed; you consume in your heat all the soul's self-love; you are the fire which takes away cold; with your light you illuminate me so that I may know all your truth. Clothe me, clothe me with yourself, Eternal Truth, so that I may run this mortal life with true obedience, and with the light of your most holy faith.

—St. Catherine of Siena

*B*eloved Lord, Almighty God!
Through the rays of the sun,
Through the waves of the air,
Through the All-pervading Life
   in space,
Purify and revivify me, and, I pray.
Heal my body, heart, and soul.
                    Amen.

—HAZRAT INAYAT KHAN

$\mathcal{Y}$ou made me to find you; give me
strength to seek you. My strength and my
weakness are in your hands: preserve my
strength and help my weakness. Where
you have opened the door, let me enter in;
where it is shut, open to my knocking.

Let me ever increase in remembering you,
understanding you, loving you, until you
restore me to your perfect pattern.

—ST. AUGUSTINE

Give us a pure heart that we
  may see thee,
A humble heart that we may
  hear thee,
A heart of love that we may
  serve thee,
A heart of faith that we may
  love thee.

—DAG HAMMARSKJÖLD

I love you Jesus, my love,
    above all things;
I repent with my whole heart
    for having offended you.
Never permit me to separate
    myself from you again.
Grant that I may love you always
    then do with me what you will.

—THE STATIONS OF THE CROSS

From the blossoming lotus of devotion,
 at the center of my heart,
Rise up, O compassionate master,
 my only refuge!
I am plagued by past actions and
 turbulent emotions:
To protect me in my misfortune
Remain as the jewel-ornament on the
 crown of my head, the mandala of
 great bliss,
Arousing all my mindfulness and
 awareness, I pray!

—JIKMÉ LINGRA

$\mathcal{A}$s my head rests on my pillow
Let my soul rest in your mercy.

As my limbs relax on my mattress,
Let my soul relax in your peace.

As my body finds warmth beneath the
blankets,
Let my soul find warmth in your love.

As my mind is filled with dreams,
Let my soul be filled with visions of heaven.

—JOHANN FREYLINGHAUSEN

*A*nd the best prayer . . . bursts
freely forth from the heart to God,
when urgency and need put the
words into the mouth. Yea, a
prayer acceptable unto God can
be uttered without words, through
the fervent silent cry of the soul,
in sighs, longings and groanings of
the heart. . . .

—EPHRAIM PRETORIUS

*I*nto thine hand I commit
  my spirit:
thou hast redeemed me,
  O LORD God of truth.

—PSALM 31:5

*L*et the lost millions pray it in the dark!
My failure is no different from Jonah's.
We both have lacked the courage in the heart
To overcome the fear within the soul
And go ahead to any accomplishment.
Courage is what it takes and takes the more of
Because the deeper fear is so eternal.
And if I say we lift him from the floor
And lay him where you ordered him to lie
Before the cross, it is from fellow-feeling,
As if I asked for one more chance myself
To learn to say
Nothing can make injustice just but mercy.

—ROBERT FROST
A Masque of Mercy

I will lift up mine eyes unto the hills,
 from whence cometh my help.
My help cometh from the LORD,
 which made heaven and earth.
He will not suffer thy foot to be moved:
 he that keepeth thee will not slumber.
Behold, he that keepeth Israel shall neither
 slumber nor sleep.
The LORD is thy keeper: the LORD is thy
 shade upon thy right hand.

The sun shall not smite thee by day,
    nor the moon by night.
The LORD shall preserve thee from all evil:
    he shall preserve thy soul.
The LORD shall preserve thy going out and
    thy coming in from this time forth, and
        even for evermore.

—PSALM 121

$\mathcal{T}$ake, O Lord, and receive
all my liberty,
my memory,
my understanding,
and my entire will,
all that I have and possess.
You have given all to me.
To you, O Lord, I return it.
All is Yours, dispose of it
wholly according to Your will.
Give me Your love and Your grace,
for this is sufficient for me.

—ST. IGNATIUS LOYOLA

O living flame of love
That wounds so tenderly
In my soul's deepest centre.
As you are no longer oppressive
Perfect your work in me if it is
   your will.
Break the web of this sweet
   encounter.

–St. John of the Cross

O Merciful God, who answerest
the poor,
    Answer us,
O Merciful God, who answerest
the lowly in spirit,
    Answer us,
O Merciful God, who answerest
the broken of heart,
    Answer us.
O Merciful God,
    Answer us.

O Merciful God,
  Have compassion.
O Merciful God,
  Redeem.
O Merciful God,
  Save.
O Merciful God, have pity upon us,
  Now,
  Speedily,
  And at a near time.

—JEWISH PRAYER FOR THE
DAY OF ATONEMENT

$\mathcal{A}$t God's door—how could I
knock now,
For I have no hand or heart
now?
You have carried heart and hand,
God!
Grant me safety, God forgive
me. . . .

—JALALUDDIN RUMI
"Evening Prayer"

$\mathcal{B}$ut give me the strength that waits upon You in silence and peace. Give me humility in which alone is rest, and deliver me from pride which is the heaviest of burdens.

—THOMAS MERTON

Precious Lord, take my hand.
Lead me on. Let me stand.
I am tired. I am weak. I am worn.
Through the storm,
Through the night,
Lead me on to the light.
Take my hand, precious Lord,
and lead me home

—AFRICAN-AMERICAN SPIRITUAL

*P*rotect me, O Lord;
My boat is so small,
And your sea is so big.

—Breton Fisherman's Prayer

O God, early in the morning I cry to you.
Help me to pray
And to concentrate my thoughts on you:
I cannot do this alone.

In me there is darkness,
But with you there is light;
I am lonely, but you do not leave me;
I am feeble in heart, but with you there
    is help;
I am restless, but with you there is peace.
In me there is bitterness, but with you
    there is patience;
I do not understand your ways,
But you know the way for me . . .

Restore me to liberty,

And enable me so to live now

That I may answer before you and

    before me.

Lord, whatever this day may bring,

Your name be praised.

—DIETRICH BONHOEFFER

O Lord give me strength
that the whole world
look to me with the eyes
of a friend. Let us ever
examine each other with
the eyes of a friend.

—YAYURVEDA

The most powerful prayer,
one well nigh omnipotent,
and the worthiest work
of all is the outcome of a
quiet mind.

—MEISTER ECKHART

God be in my head, and in my
  understanding;
God be in my eyes, and in my
  looking;
God be in my mouth, and in my
  speaking;
God be in my heart, and in my
  thinking;
God be at my end, and at my
  departing.

—Sarum Primer

$\mathcal{B}$lessèd sister, holy mother, spirit of
   the fountain, spirit of the garden,
Suffer us not to mock ourselves with
   falsehood
Teach us to care and not to care
Teach us to sit still
Even among these rocks,
Our peace in His will
And even among these rocks
Sister, mother,
And spirit of the river, spirit of the sea,
Suffer me not to be separated

And let my cry come unto Thee.

—T. S. ELIOT
"Ash Wednesday"

$\mathcal{D}$ear Pan, and all you other gods who live here, grant that I may become beautiful within, and that whatever outward things I have may be in harmony with the spirit inside me. May I understand that it is only the wise who are rich, and may I have only as much money as a temperate person needs. —Is there anything else that we can ask for, Phaedrus? For me, that prayer is enough.

—SOCRATES

If I had influence with the good fairy who is supposed to preside over the christening of all children, I should ask that her gift to each child in the world be a sense of wonder so indestructible that it would last throughout life.

—RACHEL CARSON

O Lord I ask you
In the name of Muhammad and
   his line of Progeny
To have Mercy on Muhammad
   and his posterity.
And (through them) grant me
   (also)
The light in my eyes, the true
   understanding of my faith

The (Divine) Certainty in my
  heart
The sincerity in my actions and
  peace in my mind
And spaciousness in the means
  of my living
And gratitude unto You
As long as you decide to keep
  me alive.

—MUSLIM PRAYER
"Ayat-al-Kursi"

Only a brief sleep everywhere
In man, in the green, in the cup of
   the winds.
Everyone goes home to his dead heart.

—I wish the world were still a child—
And was able to tell me how it first
   drew breath.

One time there was great piety in heaven;
The stars passed the Bible around to read.
If only I could take God's hand sometime
Or see on his finger the spinning moon.

O God, O God, how far I am from you!

—ELSE LASKER-SCHULER

Soul of Christ, sanctify me.

Body of Christ, save me.

Blood of Christ, inebriate me.

Water from the side of Christ, wash me.

Passion of Christ, strengthen me.

O good Jesus, hear me.

Within thy wounds hide me.

Permit me not to be separated from thee.

From the wicked foe defend me.

At the hour of my death call me

And bid me come to thee.

That with thy saints I may praise thee

For ever and ever.

—MEDIEVAL PRAYER
"Anima Christi"

Oh Lord,
Oh, my Lord,
Oh, my good Lord,
Keep me from sinking down.

I tell you what I mean to do,
Keep me from sinking down,
I mean to go to heaven too;
Keep me from sinking down.

—ANON.
"Keep Me from Sinking Down"

*I*n itself, prayer is simply
a reverent, conscious
openness to God full
of the desire to grow in
goodness and overcome
evil.

—WILLIAM JOHNSTON

*D*earest Lord, teach me to be generous.

Teach me to serve You as You deserve;

To give and not to count the cost;

To fight and not to heed the wounds;

To toil and not to seek reward,

Save that of knowing that

I do Your will, O God.

—St. Ignatius Loyola

$\mathcal{F}$rom the cowardice that dare not
   face new truth
From the laziness that is contented
   with half truth
From the arrogance that thinks it
   knows all truth,
Good Lord, deliver me.

—KENYAN PRAYER

I now leave, not knowing when or whether ever I may return, with a task before me greater than that which rested upon Washington. Without the assistance of that Divine Being who ever attended him, I cannot succeed. With that assistance I cannot fail. Trusting in Him who can go with me, and remain with you, and be everywhere for good, let us confidently hope that all will yet be well.

—ABRAHAM LINCOLN
Farewell Address at Springfield
February 11, 1861

$\mathcal{T}$his is our hope, this is the faith that I go back South with.

With this faith we will be able to hew out of the mountain of despair a stone of hope. With this faith we will be able to transform the jangling discords of our nation into a beautiful symphony of brotherhood.

With this faith we will be able to work together, to pray together, to struggle together, to go to jail together, to stand up for freedom together, knowing that we will be free one day. . . .

—MARTIN LUTHER KING, JR.
Speech at the Lincoln Memorial
August 28, 1963

*A*ll that we ought to have thought
and have not thought,
All that we ought to have said,
and have not said,
All that we ought to have done,
and have not done;

All that we ought not to have
thought, and yet have thought,
All that we ought not to have
spoken, and yet have spoken,

All that we ought not to have
   done, and yet have done;
For thoughts, words and works,
   pray we, O God, for forgiveness.

—PERSIAN PRAYER

*B*atter my heart, three-person'd God;
    for you
As yet but knock, breathe, shine, and seek
    to mend;
That I may rise, and stand, o'erthrow me,
    and bend
Your force, to break, blow, burn and make
    me new.
I, like an usurp'd town, to another due,
Labour to admit you, but Oh, to no end,
Reason your viceroy in me, me should
    defend,
But is captiv'd, and proves weak or untrue.

Yet dearly I love you, and would be
    loved fain,
But am betroth'd unto your enemy:
Divorce me, untie, or break that knot
    again,
Take me to you, imprison me, for I
Except you enthral me, never shall be free,
Nor ever chaste, except you ravish me.

—JOHN DONNE
"Sonnet XIV"

I come before thee as one of thy many
children. See, I am small and weak;
I need thy strength and wisdom.
Grant me to walk in beauty and that my
eyes may ever behold the crimson
sunset. May my hands treat with
respect the things which thou hast
created, may my ears hear thy voice!
Make me wise, that I may understand
the things which thou hast taught my
people, which thou hast hidden in every
leaf and every rock.

I long for strength, not in order that I
    may overreach my brother but to fight
    my greatest enemy—myself.
Make me ever ready to come to thee with
    pure hands and candid eyes, so that
    my spirit, when life disappears like the
    setting sun, may stand unashamed
    before thee.

—SIOUX PRAYER

Great Spirit, Great Spirit,
   my Grandfather,
all over the earth the faces of living
   things are all alike.
With tenderness have these come
   up out of the ground.
Look upon these faces of children
   without number
and with children in their arms,
that they may face the winds
and walk the good road to the day
   of quiet.

—BLACK ELK

$\mathcal{N}$ow I lay me down to sleep,
I pray the Lord my soul to keep;
If I should die before I wake,
I pray the Lord my soul to take.

—A CHILD'S EVENING PRAYER

Cold, slow, silent, but returning,
   after so many hours.
The sight of something outside
   me, the day is breaking.
May salt, this one day, be sharp
   upon my tongue;
May I sleep, this one night,
   without waking.

—RANDALL JARRELL
"A Prayer at Morning"

Lord, I believe;
help thou mine unbelief.

—MARK 9:24

My Lord, I do not
believe. Help thou mine
unbelief.

—SAMUEL BUTLER

Wild Nights—Wild Nights!
Were I with thee
Wild Nights should be
Our luxury!

Futile—the Winds—
To a Heart in port—
Done with the Compass—
Done with the Chart!

Rowing in Eden—
Ah, the Sea!
Might I but moor—Tonight—
In Thee!

—EMILY DICKINSON

$\mathcal{L}$ord, kind today but brutal
  yesterday,
Lord of two faces—vengefulness
  and love—
I toss you, just like dice tossed in
  the wind,
my prayer of blasphemy and
  praise!

—Antonio Machado
"The Iberian God"

Open your doors to us, O Lord.
The day goes down; the sun falls,
the sun disappears. Eternal, we
come to your doors. We implore
you: Pardon us. We implore you:
Have mercy upon us. Save us!

—NIKOS KAZANTZAKIS
The Last Temptation of Christ

The noblest prayer is that,
when he who prays
Is inwardly transformed to
that he kneels before.

—Angelus Silesius

God, I offer myself to Thee—
to build with me and to do with
me as Thou wilt. Relieve me of
the bondage of self, that I may
better do Thy will. Take away my
difficulties, that victory over them
may bear witness to those I would
help of Thy Power, Thy Love,
and Thy Way of life. May I do
Thy will always!

—ALCOHOLICS ANONYMOUS

O Lord Jesus Christ
who art as the shadow of a great rock in
    a weary land,
who beholdest thy weak creatures
weary of labour, weary of pleasure,
weary of hope deferred, weary of self,
in thine abundant compassion,
and fellow feeling with us,
and unutterable tenderness,
bring us we pray thee,
unto thy rest.

— CHRISTINA ROSSETTI
"In Weariness"

O Savior, as thou hang'st upon the tree;
I turn my back to thee, but to receive
Corrections, till thy mercies bid thee leave.
O think me worth thine anger, punish me,
Burn off my rusts, and my deformity,
Restore thine image, so much, by thy
   grace,
That thou may'st know me, and I'll turn
   my face.

—JOHN DONNE
"Good Friday, 1613. Riding Westward."

O God,

If I am raw, cook me!

If I am cooked, burn me!

—Kwaja Abdullah Ansari

Lord, let Your light be only for the day,
And the darkness for the night.
And let my dress, my poor humble dress
Lie quietly over my chair at night.

Let the church-bells be silent,
My neighbour Ivan not ring them at night.
Let the wind not waken the children
Out of their sleep at night.

Let the hen sleep on its roost, the horse in
    the stable
All through the night.
Remove the stone from the middle of the road
That the thief may not stumble at night.

Let heaven be quiet during the night,
Restrain the lightning, silence the thunder,
They should not frighten mothers giving birth
To their babies at night.

And me too protect against fire and water,
Protect my poor roof at night.
Let my dress, my poor humble dress
Lie quietly over my chair at night.

—NECHUM BRONZE

$\mathcal{L}$ord, in your great generosity,
heal my sickness, wash away my
    defilement,
enlighten my blindness, enrich my poverty,
and clothe my nakedness.
May I receive the bread of angels,
the King of kings and Lord of lords,
with humble reverence,
with the purity and faith,
the repentance and love, and the
    determined purpose
that will help to bring me to salvation.

—St. Thomas Aquinas

$\mathcal{T}$he long days of our sorrow still endure;
Father, grant to the soul thou hast been
    chastening
that thou hast promised, the healing and
    the cure.
Should it be ours to drain the cup of
    grieving
even to the dregs of pain, at thy command,
we will not falter, thankfully receiving
all that is given by thy loving hand.

—DIETRICH BONHOEFFER

O Lord!
thou knowest how busy
I must be this day:
if I forget thee,
do not thou forget me.

—SIR JACOB ASTLEY

*L*ord, hear me out,
    and hear me out this
    day:
From me to Thee's
    a long and terrible way.

—THEODORE ROETHKE

At Tara today in this fateful hour
I place all heaven with its power,
And the sun with its brightness,
And the snow with its whiteness,
And fire with all the strength it has,
And lightning with its rapid wrath
And the winds with their swiftness
along the path,

And the sea with its deepness,
And the rocks with their steepness
And the Earth with its starkness,
All these I place
By God's almighty help and grace,
Between myself and the powers of
  Darkness.

—St. Patrick

$\mathcal{T}$hou, my Lord Jesus Christ, Thou who camest into the world in order to save those who were lost, Thou who didst leave the ninety and nine sheep in order to look for the lost one, look Thou for me in the path of my errors, where I hide myself from Thee and from mankind. Thou the good shepherd let me hear Thy gentle voice, let me know it, let me follow it!

—SØREN KIERKEGAARD

Wa-kon'da,

here needy he stands,

and I am he.

—OMAHA TRIBAL PRAYER

If the love You have for me Is like the love I have for You, My God, what detains me? Oh, what is delaying You?

—St. Teresa of Avila

O God who made this
beautiful earth, when
will it be ready to receive
your saints? How long,
O Lord, how long?

—George Bernard Shaw

I call to Nature, the mother of all,
   the mother who makes,
Heavenly, honored, goddess of wealth,
   sovereign,
The one who wins, who is never tamed,
   the narrator, the Giver of Light,
Stronger than the strongest, who gives
   her breasts to all,
Who never dies, the firstborn, known in
   legends, who helps us do,
Born of the night, all wisdom, carrier of
   light, a strong holder-back,
We see your footprints that whirl silently
   when you are still.

—ORPHIC HYMN

God guard me from those thoughts
   men think
In the mind alone;
He that sings a lasting song
Thinks in a marrow-bone;

From all that makes a wise old man
That can be praised of all;
O what am I that I should not seem
For the song's sake a fool?

I pray—for fashion's word is out
And prayer comes round again—
That I may seem, though I die old,
A foolish, passionate man.

—William Butler Yeats
"A Prayer for Old Age"

I believe in the sun even
　　when it is not shining.
I believe in love even when
　　feeling it not.
I believe in God even
　　when he is silent.

—JEWISH PRAYER

*A*bsolute attention is prayer.

—Zen Saying

$\mathcal{M}$y Lord God, I have no idea
where I am going. I do not see the
road ahead of me. I cannot know
for certain where it will end. Nor
do I really know myself and the
fact that I think that I am following
Your will does not mean that I am
actually doing so. But I believe
that the desire to please You does
in fact please You. And I hope that
I have that desire in all that I am
doing. I hope that I will never do
anything apart from that desire.

And I know that if I do this,
You will lead me by the right
road though I may know nothing
about it. Therefore will I trust
You always though I may seem to
be lost and in the shadow of death.
I will not fear, for You are ever
with me, and You will never leave
me to face my perils alone.

—THOMAS MERTON

*T*he way I must enter
leads through darkness to
   darkness—
O moon above the mountains' rim,
please shine a little further
   on my path.

—Izumi Shikibu

O shooting star

that fell into my eyes and

   through my body—:

Not to forget you.

   To endure.

—Rainer Maria Rilke
"Death"

God of our life,

there are days when the burdens we carry

chafe our shoulders and weigh us down;

when the road seems dreary and endless,

the skies gray and threatening;

when our lives have no music in them,

and our hearts are lonely,

and our souls have lost their courage.

Flood the path with light,

run our eyes to where

the skies are full of promise;

tune our hearts to brave music;
give us the sense of comradeship
with heroes and saints of every age;
and so quicken our spirits
that we may be able to encourage
the souls of all who journey with us
on the road of life, to your honor and glory.

—ST. AUGUSTINE

God grant me the
serenity to accept the things
   I cannot change;
courage to change the things
   I can;
and wisdom to know the
   difference.

Living one day at a time;
Enjoying one moment at a time;
Accepting hardships as the pathway
   to peace;

Taking this sinful world as it is,
  not as I would have it;
Trusting that you will make all
  things right if I surrender
    to your will;
That I may be reasonably happy
  in this life
And supremely happy with you
  forever in the next.

—ATTRIBUTED TO REINHOLD NIEBUHR

*B*eloved, let us love one another: for love is of God; and every one that loveth is born of God, and knoweth God. He that loveth not knoweth not God; for God is love.

—1 John 4:7

$\mathcal{A}$lmighty and everlasting God, who art
always more ready to hear than we to pray,
and art wont to give more than either we
desire, or deserve: Pour down upon us the
abundance of thy mercy; forgiving us those
things whereof our conscience is afraid, and
giving us those good things which we are
not worthy to ask, but through the merits
and mediation of Jesus Christ, thy Son,
our Lord. Amen.

—THE BOOK OF COMMON PRAYER

Silent friend of many distances, feel
how your breath enlarges all of space.
Let your presence ring out like a bell
into the night. What feeds upon your face

grows mighty from the nourishment thus
offered. Move through transformation, out
and in. What is the deepest loss that you
have suffered? If drinking is bitter, change
yourself to wine.

In this immeasurable darkness, be the power
that rounds your senses in their magic ring,
the sense of their mysterious encounter.

And if the earthly no longer knows your name,
whisper to the silent earth: I'm flowing.
To the flashing water say: I am.

—RAINER MARIA RILKE
The Sonnets to Orpheus

We wait in the darkness!
  Come, all ye who listen,
    Help in our night journey:
    Now no sun is shining;
    Now no star is glowing;
    Come show us the pathway:
    The night is not friendly;
  The moon has forgot us,
We wait in the darkness!

—Iroquois Prayer

$\mathcal{H}$ow many nights
have I lain in terror,
O Creator Spirit, Maker of night and day,

only to walk out
the next morning over the frozen world
hearing under the creaking of snow
faint, peaceful breaths . . .
snake,
bear, earthworm, ant . . .

and above me
a wild crow crying *'yaw yaw yaw'*
from a branch nothing cried from ever in
my life.

—GALWAY KINNELL
"How Many Nights"

I know that thou canst do every thing, and that no thought can be withholden from thee.

Who is he that hideth counsel without knowledge? therefore have I uttered that I understood not; things too wonderful for me, which I knew not.

Hear, I beseech thee, and I will speak: I will demand of thee, and declare thou unto me.

I have heard of thee by the hearing of the ear: but now mine eye seeth thee.

Wherefore I abhor myself, and repent in dust and ashes.

—JOB 42:2–6

ABOUT PRAYER

What does it matter how
I pray, so long as my
prayers are answered?

—Sitting Bull

Raise me up, Lord, who am fallen down,
void of love and fear and faith and awe;
I long to rise and in my place abide;
mine is the longing, mine the impediment.

Between thy might and mercy I am torn;
in others every day I see amend,
in me I see fresh longing to offend thee.

—MIGUEL DE GUEVARA
"Raise Me Up, Lord"

I am here abroad,
I am here in need,
I am here in pain,
I am here in straits,
I am here alone.
O God, aid me.

— CELTIC CHARM

Grandfather,
Look at our brokenness.

We know that in all creation
Only the human family
Has strayed from the Sacred Way.

We know that we are the ones
Who are divided
And we are the ones
Who must come back together
To walk in the Sacred Way.

Grandfather,
Sacred One,
Teach us love, compassion, and honor
That we may heal the earth
And heal each other.

— OJIBWA PRAYER

$\mathcal{M}$y Lord and my Creator,
   you bear with me and nourish me—
      be my helper.
I thirst for you, I hunger for you,
   I desire you, I sigh for you, I covet you:
I am like an orphan deprived of the
   presence of a very kind father,
who, weeping and wailing, does not cease
   to cling to the dear face with his whole
      heart.
I want you, I hope for you, I seek you;
'to you my heart has said, seek my face';
'your face, Lord, have I sought;
   turn not your face from me.'

—St. Anselm

*W*ilt Thou forgive that sin where I begun,

    Which is my sin, though it were done before?

Wilt Thou forgive that sin, through which I run,

    And do run still: though still I do deplore?

       When Thou hast done, Thou has not done,

        For, I have more.

—JOHN DONNE
"A Hymn to God the Father"

If anyone has hurt me or harmed me
knowingly or unknowingly in thought,
word, or deed, I freely forgive them.

And I too ask forgiveness if I have hurt
anyone or harmed anyone knowingly or
unknowingly in thought, word, or deed.

> May I be happy
> May I be peaceful
> May I be free
>
> May my friends be happy
> May my friends be peaceful
> May my friends be free

Hear my prayer, O LORD, and let
my cry come unto thee.
Hide not thy face from me in the
day when I am in trouble; incline
thine ear unto me: in the day
when I call answer me speedily.
My days are like a shadow that
declineth; and I am withered like
grass.

—PSALM 102:1–2, 11

Out of the depths have I cried unto thee,
   O LORD.
LORD, hear my voice: let thine ears be
   attentive to the voice of my supplications.
If thou, LORD, shouldest mark iniquities,
   O LORD, who shall stand?
But there is forgiveness with thee, that thou
   mayest be feared.
I wait for the LORD, my soul doth wait, and
   in his word do I hope.
My soul waiteth for the LORD more than they
   that watch for the morning: I say, more
   than they that watch for the morning.
Let Israel hope in the LORD: for with the
   LORD there is mercy, and with him is
   plenteous redemption.
And he shall redeem Israel from all his
   iniquities.

—PSALM 130

This time, I have left my body behind me, crying

In its dark thorns.

Still,

There are good things in this world.

It is dusk.

It is the good darkness

Of women's hands that touch loaves.

The spirit of a tree begins to move.

I touch leaves.

I close my eyes, and think of water.

—JAMES WRIGHT
"Trying to Pray"

*I*n a corrupt age,
when prayers are not
answered,
that itself is the answer.

—Muso Kokushi

$\mathcal{T}$here is nothing I can give you
Which you do not have; but there
is much, very much, that while I
cannot give it, you can take.

No heaven can come to us unless
our hearts find rest in today. Take
heaven! No peace lies in the future
which is not hidden in this present
instant. Take peace!

The gloom of the world is but a shadow. Behind it, yet within reach, is joy. There is radiance and glory in the darkness, could we but see, and to see, we have only to look. I beseech you to look

—FRA GIOVANNI

$\mathcal{A}$nd Jesus saith to his disciples, "Sit ye here, while I shall pray." And he went forward a little, and fell on the ground, and prayed that, if it were possible, the hour might pass from him.

And he said, "Ab'-ba, Father, all things are possible unto thee; take away this cup from me: nevertheless not what I will, but what thou wilt."

— MARK 14:32b, 35–36

I am not eager, bold
Or strong—all that is past.
I am ready not to do,
At last, at last!

—St. Peter Canisius

*B*ow, stubborn knees!

—WILLIAM SHAKESPEARE
Hamlet

$\mathcal{Y}$our prayer should be,
  "Break the legs
of what I want to happen.
  Humiliate
my desire. Eat me like candy.
It's spring, and finally
I have no will."

—JELALUDDIN RUMI

$\mathcal{Y}$ou hear the long roll of the plunging
    ground,
The whistle of stones, the quail's cry in
    the grass.
I stammer like a bird, I rasp like stone,
I mutter, with gray hands upon my face.
The earth blurs, beyond me, into dark.
Spinning in such bewildered sleep, I need
To know you, whirring above me,
    when I wake.
Come down. Come down. I lie afraid.
I have lain alien in my self so long,
How can I understand love's angry
    tongue?

—JAMES WRIGHT
"A Prayer in My Sickness"

There is no life without prayer. Without prayer there is only madness and horror.

—Vasili Rozanov

*I*n spite of everything, I still believe
that people are really good at heart.
I simply can't build up my hopes on
    a foundation
consisting of confusion, misery, and death.
I see the world gradually being turned into
    a wilderness,
I hear the ever-approaching thunder,
    which will destroy us, too,
I can feel the suffering of millions, and yet,
if I look up into the heavens,
I think that it will all come right,
that this cruelty will end,
and that peace and tranquility will return
    again.

—ANNE FRANK

$\mathcal{D}$eliver me from my own
shadows, my Lord, from
the wrecks and confusion
of my days.

—RABINDRANATH TAGORE

$\mathcal{T}$o God: to illuminate all men. Beginning with Skid Road.

Let Occidental and Washington be transformed into a higher place, the plaza of eternity.

Illuminate the welders in shipyards with the brilliance of their torches.

Let the crane operator lift up his arm for joy.

Let elevators creak and speak, ascending and descending in awe.

Let the mercy of the flower's direction beckon in the eye.

Let the straight flower bespeak its
purpose in straightness—to seek the light.

Let the crooked flower bespeak its
purpose in crookedness—to seek the light.

Let the crookedness and straightness
bespeak the light.

Let Puget Sound be a blast of light.

I feed on your Name like a cockroach
on a crumb—this cockroach is holy.

—ALLEN GINSBERG
"Psalm III"

*L*isten

with the night falling we are saying thank you
we are stopping on the bridges to bow from the
railings
we are running out of the glass rooms
with our mouths full of food to look at the sky
and say thank you
we are standing by the water looking out
in different directions

back from a series of hospitals back from a
mugging
after funerals we are saying thank you
after the news of the dead
whether or not we knew them we are saying
thank you
looking up from tables we are saying thank you
in a culture up to its chin in shame
living in the stench it has chosen we are saying
thank you

over telephones we are saying thank you
in doorways and in the backs of cars and
in elevators
remembering wars and the police at the
back door
and the beatings on stairs we are saying thank you
in the banks that use us we are saying thank you
with the crooks in office with the rich
and fashionable
unchanged we go on saying thank you thank you

with the animals dying around us
our lost feelings we are saying thank you
with the forests falling faster than the minutes
of our lives we are saying thank you
with the words going out like cells of a brain
with the cities growing over us like the earth
we are saying thank you faster and faster
with nobody listening we are saying thank you
we are saying thank you and waving
dark though it is

—W. S. MERWIN

Mother of gods, father of gods,
Ancient God,
A mere appendage of the realm,
a common man, has come.
He comes crying, he comes in
sadness, he comes with guilt.
Perhaps he has slipped, perhaps
he has stumbled, perhaps he
has touched the bird of evil, the
spider's web, the tuft of thorns:

It wounds his heart, it troubles
   him.
Master, Lord,
Ever Present, Ever Near,
Take it from him: hear the pain of
   this common man.

—Aztec Prayer

The Road goes ever on and on
   Down from the door where it began.
Now far ahead the Road has gone,
   And I must follow, if I can,
Pursuing it with eager feet,
   Until it joins some larger way
Where many paths and errands meet.
   And whither then? I cannot say.

—J.R.R. TOLKIEN

Sunset and evening star,
  And one clear call for me!
And may there be no moaning of the bar,
  When I put out to sea.

For though from out our bourne of time
    and place
  The flood may bear me far,
I hope to see my pilot face to face
  When I have crossed the bar.

—ALFRED, LORD TENNYSON
"Crossing the Bar"

$\mathcal{H}$ail to you gods . . .

   On that day of the great reckoning.

   Behold me, I have come to you,

   Without sin, without guilt, without evil,

   Without a witness against me,

   Without one whom I have wronged. . . .

   Rescue me, protect me,

   Do not accuse me before the great god!

   I am one pure of mouth, pure of hands.

                              — THE BOOK OF THE DEAD

Sometimes a man stands up during supper and walks outdoors, and keeps on walking, because of a church that stands somewhere in the East.

And his children say blessings on him as if he were dead.

And another man, who remains inside his own house, stays there, inside the dishes and in the glasses, so that his children have to go far out into the world toward that same church, which he forgot.

— RAINER MARIA RILKE

*A*bide with me: fast falls the
    eventide;
The darkness deepens; Lord,
    with me abide;
When other helpers fail, and
    comforts flee,
Help of the helpless, O abide
    with me.

—HENRY FRANCIS LYTE
"Eventide"

I have gone forward with
Some, a few lonely some.
They have fallen to death.
I die with them.
Lord, I have loved Thy cursed,
The beauty of Thy house:
Come down. Come down.
Why dost Thou hide thy face?

—JAMES WRIGHT
"Speak"

$\mathcal{A}$t a certain point you say to the woods,
to the sea, to the mountains, the world,
Now I am ready. Now I will stop and be
wholly attentive. You empty yourself and
wait, listening. After a time you hear it:
there is nothing there. There is nothing but
those things only, those created objects,
discrete, growing or holding, or swaying,
being rained on or raining, held, flooding
or ebbing, standing, or spread. You feel the
world's word as a tension, a hum, a single
chorused note everywhere the same. This is
it: this hum is the silence.

The silence is all there is. It is the alpha
and the omega. It is God's brooding over
the face of the waters; it is the blended note
of the ten thousand things, the whine of
wings. You take a step in the right direction
to pray to this silence, and even to address
the prayer to "World." Distinctions blur.
Quit your tents. Pray without ceasing.

—ANNIE DILLARD

*H*ow many nights must it take
   one such as me to learn
   that we aren't, after all, made
   from that bird which flies out of its ashes,
   that for a man
   as he goes up in flames, his one work
   is
   to open himself, to be
   the flames?

—GALWAY KINNELL

O God, the night has passed and the day has dawned. How I long to know if Thou hast accepted my prayers or if Thou hast rejected them. Therefore console me for it is Thine to console this state of mine. Thou hast given me life and cared for me, and Thine is the glory. If Thou want to drive me from Thy door, yet would I not forsake it, for the love that I bear in my heart towards Thee.

— RABI'A

*L*ead, kindly Light, amid the encircling
   gloom,
Lead thou me on;
The night is dark, and I am far from home,
Lead thou me on.
Keep thou my feet; I do not ask to see
The distant scene; one step enough for me.

I was not ever thus, nor prayed that thou
Shouldst lead me on;
I loved to choose and see my path; but now
Lead thou me on.
I loved the garish day, and, spite of fears,
Pride ruled my will: remember not past years.

So long thy power hath blest me, sure it still
Will lead me on
O'er moor and fen, o'er crag and torrent, till
The night is gone,
And with the morn those Angel faces smile,
Which I have loved long since, and lost awhile.

—JOHN HENRY NEWMAN
"Lead, Kindly Light"

When the spent sun throws up its rays
    on cloud
And goes down burning into the gulf below,
No voice in nature is heard to cry aloud
At what has happened. Birds, at least,
    must know
It is the change to darkness in the sky.
Murmuring something quiet in her breast,
One bird begins to close a faded eye;
Or overtaken too far from his nest,
Hurrying low above the grove, some waif
Swoops just in time to his remembered tree.

At most he thinks or twitters softly, "Safe!
Now let the night be dark for all of me.
Let the night be too dark for me to see
Into the future. Let what will be, be."

—ROBERT FROST
"Acceptance"

I want to die easy when I die.
I want to die easy when I die.
Shout salvation as I fly,
I want to die easy when I die.

—AFRICAN-AMERICAN SPIRITUAL

May the Father take you
In his fragrant clasp
of love,
When you go across the
flooding streams
And the black river
of death.

—CELTIC BLESSING

When the signs of age begin to mark
    my body
(and still more when they touch my mind);
when the ill that is to diminish me or carry
    me off strikes from without
or is born within me;
when the painful moment comes in which
    I suddenly waken
to the fact that I am ill or growing old;
and above all at the last moment
when I feel I am losing hold of myself
and am absolutely passive in the hands

of the great unknown forces that have
    formed me;
in all those dark moments, O God,
grant that I may understand that it is you
(provided only my faith is strong enough)
who are painfully parting the fibers of
    my being
in order to penetrate to the very marrow
    of my substance
and bear me away within yourself.

—TEILHARD DE CHARDIN

Grandfather, Great
Father, let matters go
well with me, for I am
going into the forest.

—Bambuti Pygmy Prayer

*I*f a dead person were
allowed to return to this
world and pray, you can
be sure that he would pray
with all his might.

—RABBI NACHMAN OF BRATSLO

From delusion lead me
   to Truth.
From darkness lead me
   to Light.
From death lead me
   to Immortality.

—THE UPANISHADS

*L*ord! can't you see I'm weary
Of this rising and dying and living.
Take it all, but once more bring
    me close
To sense the freshness of this
    crimson rose.

—ANNA AKHMATOVA
"Last Rose"

*A*nd if tonight my soul may find
   her peace
in sleep, and sink in good oblivion,
and in the morning wake like a
   new-opened flower
then I have been dipped again in
   God, and new-created.

–D. H. LAWRENCE

God bless us every one!

—CHARLES DICKENS
"Tiny Tim's Prayer"

A SELECTIVE GUIDE

$\mathcal{F}$or those who wish, we offer the following highly selective list of prayers, arranged by topic, time of day, or particular need. Of course, the interpretation of prayer is very personal, so please view this guide only as a starting point.

INDEX

*A*sterisked page numbers indicate the ABOUT PRAYER features.

ACKNOWLEDGMENTS

We gratefully acknowledge the following for permission to reprint material copyrighted or controlled by them. Every effort has been made to clear reprints. If any required credits have been omitted or any rights overlooked, it is completely unintentional, and we will gladly correct any omissions in future reprints.

♦Excerpt from p. 63 of *Alcoholics Anonymous*. Reprinted with permission. ♦Lyrics from "Father of Night" by Bob Dylan. Copyright © 1970 by Big Sky Music. All rights reserved. International copyright secured. Used by permission. ♦"Owning Everything" written by Leonard Cohen. Copyright © 1961 by Leonard Cohen. Used by permission. All rights reserved. ♦"Human Wisdom" by Charles Peguy from *Short Prayers for the Long Day*, compiled by Giles & Melville Harcourt. Published by Collins, 1978. ♦"Song to the Creator" by St. Hildegard of Bingen. Reprinted from St. Hildegard of Bingen: Symposia, A Critical Edition of the Symphonia armonie celestium revelationum, ed./transl. Barbara Newman. Copyright © 1989 by Cornell University. By permission of the publisher, Cornell University Press. ♦Excerpts from *Celtic Prayer*, transl. Alexander Carmichael, ed. Trace Murphy. An Image Book published by Doubleday, a division of Bantam Doubleday Dell Publishing Group, Inc., 1996. ♦Lines from "The Marrow" from *The Collected Works of Theodore Roethke* by Theodore Roethke. Copyright © 1964 by Beatrice Roethke, Administratrix of the Estate of Theodore Roethke. By permission of Doubleday, a division of Bantam Doubleday Dell Publishing Group, Inc., and Faber and Faber, Ltd. ♦Excerpt from *Goodnight Willie Lee, I'll See You in The Morning* by Alice Walker. Copyright © 1975 by Alice Walker. By permission of Doubleday, a division of Bantam Doubleday Dell Publishing Group, Inc., and Wendy Weil Agency. ♦Excerpt from "A Prayer at Morning" from *The Complete Poems* by Randall Jarrell. Copyright © 1969 by Mrs. Randall Jarrell. By permission of Farrar, Straus & Giroux and Faber and Faber, Ltd. ♦Excerpts from *Thoughts in Solitude* by Thomas Merton. Copyright © 1956, 1958 by the Abbey of Gethsemani, copyright renewed 1986. Published by Farrar, Straus & Giroux.